The Labour Party and the Organization of Secondary Education 1918-65

LIBRARY OF POLITICAL STUDIES

GENERAL EDITOR:

H. VICTOR WISEMAN
Professor of Government
University of Exeter

The Labour Party and the Organization of Secondary Education 1918-65

by Michael Parkinson
*Department of Political Theory and Institutions,
University of Liverpool*

LONDON
ROUTLEDGE & KEGAN PAUL

*First published 1970
by Routledge & Kegan Paul Ltd
Broadway House, 68-74 Carter Lane
London EC4
Printed in Great Britain by
Northumberland Press Limited, Gateshead
© Michael Parkinson 1970
No part of this book may be reproduced
in any form without permission from
the publisher, except for the quotation
of brief passages in criticism*

ISBN 0 7100 6767 4

Contents

	General editor's introduction	page vii
1	Introduction	1
2	Secondary education for all, 1918–44	6
	The 1918 Fisher Education Act	6
	The Advisory Committee on Education and post-war policies	9
	Recession in education	13
	'Secondary Education for All'	14
	Labour in office, 1923	17
	The Hadow Report	21
	The second minority Labour Government	23
	Retrenchment again	27
	The 1936 Education Act	29
	The development of multilateralism	31
	The 1944 Education Act	33
3	The Labour Government, 1945–51	36
	The prospects for reform	36
	Tripartitism and Party dissent	38
	The Ministry and grammar schools	41
	Continuity under the new Minister	42
	Internal confusion and criticism intensified	43
	The Minister fails to convince his critics	45
	An explanation of the controversy	47
	The confusion about the implications of secondary education for all	47
	The educational basis of tripartitism	49
	The administrative problems	51
4	Selection and segregation in English secondary education	54

CONTENTS

	Ideological aspects of comprehensivism	55
	Educational objections to tripartitism	57
	The evidence of sociologists	60
	Objections to selection and segregation	64
	The structure of ability	65
	Social-class factors in educational selection	66
	The failures of the selective system	68
5	The Labour Party and the comprehensive school, 1951–65	71
	Reappraisal of the Labour administration	71
	The new proposals and their critics	72
	The Conservatives' view of comprehensives	75
	Problems of presenting the policy to the electorate	76
	Strategies for implementing the policies	80
	Retreat from rigour	84
	National deadlock	87
	The Labour Government	89
6	Labour and private education	94
	Early Party opposition	94
	The failure to act	96
	The issue reopened	98
	The Fleming Report and Party reaction	102
	The Labour Government	104
	Return to Opposition and reappraisal	107
	The conflict intensifies	110
	The need for action accepted	115
	The Labour Government and the Public Schools Commission	116
7	Conclusion	119
	Suggestions for further reading	129
	Bibliography	131

General editor's introduction

This series is designed primarily to meet the needs of students of government, politics, or political science in universities and other institutions providing courses leading to degrees. Each volume aims to provide a brief general introduction indicating the significance of its topic, e.g. executives, parties, pressure-groups, etc., and then a longer 'case study' relevant to the general topic. First-year students will thus be introduced to the kind of detailed work on which all generalizations must be based, while more mature students will have an opportunity to become acquainted with recent original research in a variety of fields. The series will eventually provide a comprehensive coverage of most aspects of political science in a more interesting manner than in the large volume which often fails to compensate by breadth what it inevitably lacks in depth.

Many studies of political parties have been published, but, as Mr. Parkinson points out, very few of them have been concerned with parties as policy-makers. Interest has been focused on parties as organizations, and the current belief in 'the end of ideology' has tended to divert interest from the ideas and purposes of political parties. In this case study Mr. Parkinson examines the attitude of the Labour Party towards the organization of secondary education, and in particular to comprehensive schools. He

GENERAL EDITOR'S INTRODUCTION

shows that the general philosophy of the Labour Party necessarily implies a profound belief in the social importance of education, although there has been by no means a uniformity of thought as to the implications of this for secondary education. The story he tells covers the period from 1918 to 1965, and is an essential background to the current controversies about comprehensive education. He makes the useful point that political parties may be influential, not only when they are in office and able to implement their policies, but that they may also exercise an indirect influence over the course of events. This was, of course, a point which Lord Attlee made in correspondence with Professor Laski, and Mr. Parkinson's case study will illustrate how such 'pressure-group' activities may be significant. The monograph will undoubtedly be regarded as an important contribution to one aspect of the study of political parties in the United Kingdom.

H.V.W.

(Professor Wiseman had written this introduction before his death in November, 1969.)

1
Introduction

This book is primarily a case study which examines the education policies of a single political party in a limited historical context. For this reason, its conclusions cannot be generalized far beyond this particular study. Any claim to significance it may have rests solely on the importance of the issues examined. Nevertheless, one general conclusion may be drawn from it. It relates to the way in which political parties are studied.

Parties can play a variety of roles within the political system. They represent social groups, manage political conflict, recruit political leaders, socialize political activists and mobilize public opinion. The precise functions they fulfil clearly differ between political systems and at different periods within the same system. However, one of the most crucial and enduring functions of parties, of vital concern to the political scientist, is the role they play in aggregating public demands and interests, more simply in developing public policies for governing the community in which they exist. Yet it can be argued that this important aspect of party activity has to some extent been neglected by much contemporary research. One can illustrate this point by citing some of the more prominent recent studies of political parties.

Duverger's work on political parties, for example, which probably did most to reawaken academic interest in the area, does not deal with the policy-making process in parties. It had two major concerns. First, it examined some of the organizational characteristics of modern parties, and, second, it looked at ways in which the study of different types of party systems could be used as a starting-point for the analysis of the total political system, thus treating party as an important explanatory phenomenon rather than as an object of enquiry for itself. This latter approach has been widely employed in the study of American parties, with parties and the party system treated as the best introduction to the understanding of American government and politics rather than as a source of interest for their own sake. The leading work on British political parties by Robert McKenzie, which is more like a case study, is rather different in style, but this too does not directly deal with problems of policy-making. It concentrates primarily on the organizational features of British parties, and while these do obviously impinge on aspects of the policy process, its essential concern is for the internal distribution of power within the respective parties. Similarly, one could make the point that the most coherent study of British local parties by Bulpitt primarily concerns itself with the conditions under which local parties operate, but rarely with their policy characteristics. Finally, one can see that the expanding number of studies devoted to the analysis of the internal sociology of political parties, which are probably best characterized by the work of Eldersveld, despite their individual merits, often neglect direct consideration of the policy-making processes.

These brief comments are not intended to question the value of either these individual pieces of research or the general approaches they reveal to the study of political parties. Rather they are meant to indicate the rather surprising absence of studies dealing with the dynamics

INTRODUCTION

of the policy-making processes in political parties, and to suggest that there is a great deal of scope for case studies or more general studies on this topic to complement our knowledge of party activity in other areas. It is in this context that this present study may prove useful.

This argument does, of course, presuppose that parties do develop policies, with which they can be associated and to which they are committed over a period of time. It is therefore slightly different from Downs's view of parties which sees their prime function as merely to gain office by seeking the combination of policies which will ensure the maximum electoral support. It also differs from that more recently outlined by Leon Epstein, which treats parties simply as a collection of leaders who, once in office, will attempt to resolve the issues which arise as efficiently as possible, but entirely on a pragmatic, *ad hoc* basis. Our view would stress that political parties, because of the role they have to play, can, at least at certain stages in their career, be characterized by general policy orientations which will predispose them to act in relatively predictable ways and which will allow them to be differentiated from their political opponents. Obviously the stability consistency and coherence of policies will differ between different parties, and this case study of the Labour Party policies for secondary education should throw light on some of these issues at least in an important policy area.

Before entering into the detailed analysis of party policies, however, it may be appropriate to make a few general comments on the way in which the Labour Party has traditionally regarded the issue of education. In fact, it is clear that the Party has always claimed to have recognized the value and importance of education and to have had a special concern for its interest. Indeed, G. D. H. Cole has written: 'There can be no practical socialist educational policy except in conjunction with a general policy making for social equality in every part of the structure of the communal life. That is why socialist educational ideas are so difficult to entangle from general socialist conceptions of human relations in other fields.' And in similar vein Brian Simon has stressed that the whole Labour movement's attempt to change the working classes' conception of themselves and their role in society has made it essentially 'educative in its widest sense'. Given the nature of the Labour Party and of the educational process, this alleged concern for education is not difficult to understand for a number of reasons.

For example, the process of education can be directly related to the Party's principal ethical goal of equality in at least two important ways. In the first case the Party has always emphasized that education should be seen as a moral good in itself, crucial to the development of the individual personality, and as such ought to be made equally available to all children by right, regardless of such extraneous factors as social class, and, with certain reservations, regardless of intellectual ability. At the same time the Party has been concerned that educational opportunities be equally available to all not only because of their moral worth, but also because of the direct social and economic importance of education in contemporary society. At least in this century, the English educational structure has played a crucial role in occupational and hence social selection, and has thus exercised an enormous effect on the life chances of individuals and groups in society. Naturally, the Labour Party has recognized this fact, and has been anxious that the principle of equality of opportunity for all individuals and social groups should operate in this area of social arrangements which so directly affects the distribution of social and economic rewards.

INTRODUCTION

The Party's general concern for education has been heightened for another related reason. It has traditionally been a social-democratic Party, dedicated to the idea of reform rather than revolution, and hence more interested in social engineering than violent change. And the educational process, which is at least at one level concerned with socialization and the problems of social change and social control, is an extremely important technique of social engineering. Thus in Labour Party philosophy, the education system, far from being in Marxist terms merely an element in the ideological superstructure helping to perpetuate the ascendancy of the ruling class, has become a critical tool in the attempt to reform capitalist society from within. It has been seen as an agent of peaceful social change which can facilitate a more equitable distribution of social rewards as well as a revision of social values. Thus R. H. Tawney, the most important Labour educationalist, once observed that all socialists concerned with problems of social change should ask themselves 'whether the possibility of rebuilding a tolerable civilization does not depend . . . on the deliberate cultivation of human faculties of which the proper name is education'. And, of course, the socialist view of personality, which emphasizes acquired rather than inherited characteristics and stresses the possibilities of human development in the correct social environment, has similarly led the Labour Party to value the social role of education.

Having made these few general points about the Party's theoretical concern for education, we can now go on to see whether and how this concern has revealed itself in a practical way through an analysis of its policies for the organization of English secondary education in the period 1918-65.

2
Secondary education for all, 1918-44

The 1918 Fisher Education Act

In 1918 the English education system was highly selective, elitist and class-orientated. Despite the proliferation of institutions, the State basically offered two kinds of education. The secondary schools, which provided an academic, grammar-school-type education, were attended mainly by middle-class children whose parents could afford to pay the compulsory fees. The elementary schools, which were free, were attended primarily by children from the working classes, and they provided a semi-vocational education. The secondary schools were superior to elementary schools in terms of their physical condition, e.g. size and equipment, the qualifications of the teaching staff, the salaries paid to the teaching staff, the nature of the education they offered, the leaving age for their pupils, and the kind of formal qualifications they offered and hence the occupational strata into which they sent their pupils. The secondary schools received their pupils at the age of eleven. They kept the majority until sixteen, and a number beyond that age who entered university. Mostly their pupils entered professional or clerical occupations. The elementary schools recruited their pupils at the age of five and kept them until thirteen, the minimum compulsory leaving age, and for the most part sent their children into manual occupations. A means of entry to the secondary sector from the elementary schools did exist for working-class children. The most intelligent of them could win scholarships or free places. The Board of Education had in 1907 created the free place system whereby 25% of secondary school places had to be offered to children from elementary schools, with no fees charged. But many working-class children, even when relieved of the burden of tuition fees, were not able to accept secondary places because of the other costs involved and because it meant their families forgoing the wages they could earn.

The system had, in fact, been improved since 1833, when the first government grant of £20,000 had been made to men of goodwill who were prepared to undertake the building and maintenance of voluntary elementary schools. The Education Acts of 1870 and 1902 had admitted governmental responsibility, however limited, for the provision of elementary and secondary education respectively, and a series of minor pieces of legislation up to 1918 had improved the conditions, lessened the working hours and extended the school years of British children. But, as Curtis has observed, in 1918 'the outstanding defect as it appeared to progressive thinkers, was the narrowness of the system' (Curtis, *Education in Britain since 1900*, London, 1952, p. 68). The transfer of elementary pupils to secondary schools was negligible, and for the majority of children education started at five and ended at the age of thirteen within the same elementary school.

The 1918 Fisher Education Act, introduced at the end of a war which had intensified the demand for social reform, was intended to remedy some of the deficiencies of this system, its underlying theme being that 'children and young people shall not be debarred from receiving the benefits of education by which they are capable of profiting through inability to pay fees'. This Act provided, first, for the raising of the compulsory leaving age from thirteen to fourteen, with an enabling clause allowing a local education authority (LEA) to raise the age to fifteen in its own area if it wished. Although it was apparent that Fisher would have liked to raise the leaving age universally to fifteen, he did not think the system at that time was prepared for such a measure, and preferred an alternative scheme of continuation education. Under this arrangement, continuation schools would be created to provide a suitable education on one day a week for children between the ages of fourteen and eighteen who had left school and were working. Clearly, this would be a difficult plan for the Party to deal with, for while it offered at least some gains in terms of extended education, it could also have the effect of delaying other more significant reforms.

The passage of this Act provides us with a convenient point of entry into an analysis of Labour's policies in education. It is, in fact, quite apparent at this stage that although the Party was generally committed to the idea of educational reform, it had not developed any coherent, long-term policies. It tended to react in an *ad hoc* way to issues as they arose rather than attempting itself to force the pace of reform. For example, it could be argued that a resolution accepted at the 1907 Annual Conference demanding that 'secondary and technical education' be an essential part of every child's education meant that at that time the Party had formally committed itself to a policy of universal, compulsory secondary education. However, its behaviour during the passage of this Act would deny this interpretation. Far from criticizing the Bill for its failure to extend secondary education or for its intention to introduce the concept of continuation education, Labour MPs gave it a warm welcome. Indeed, any criticism that the Bill did not go far enough was made by Liberal MPs. The Labour spokesman on the Bill reported that 'organized

SECONDARY EDUCATION FOR ALL, 1918-44

Labour is behind this Bill', which was considered 'an essential step in the right direction'. The Parliamentary Report of the National Executive Council (NEC) to the Conference in that year did, however, offer an explanation. It pointed out that while the measure 'falls short of the minimum that is adequate to the needs of the country and the opportunity before it', it was 'so comprehensive and embodies so many things that the Labour Party had advocated for a long time, that the Party decided to content itself with very few amendments in order to help smooth its passage'. This amply demonstrates the point that at this time the Party, being weak in Parliament and lacking an overall plan, was grateful to accept any reforms, however piecemeal, that would improve education.

The Advisory Committee on Education and post-war policies

But in 1918 there was a development which would at least partially change this situation. The new Party constitution published that year created a number of advisory policy committees, one of which was the Advisory Committee on Education (ACE). The significance of this Committee was that it was a small body of MPs, with powers to co-opt members and with some research facilities, dedicated to a single specific area of policy. It thus represented a clear advance on the existing machinery, a triad of the parliamentary party (PLP), the Annual Conference and NEC, giving education a legitimate and coherent spokesman in Party policy discussions. Its role was, first, to act as an advice bureau for MPs and, second, to advise on the development of long-term Party policy in education. The issues it was initially directed to work upon give a clear indication of what the Party considered were the main deficiencies of the education structure at this time. First, it was to examine the nature of the relationship between elementary and secondary schools, an area to become of critical importance a little later. Second, it was to consider and advise upon the nature and role of continuation schools. And, finally, it was to consider the system of scholarships and maintenance allowances available in the secondary sector. The Committee was soon to give a sharpness and depth to Party policy on all three issues.

In the same year the Party published *Labour and the New Social Order*, a definitive account of its post-war policies. Calling for a 'genuine rationalization of education' as 'the first step to social reconstruction in the ridding of class distinctions and privileges', this catalogued Labour's grievances with the existing structure. It stressed that the Party could not be satisfied with a system which 'condemns the great bulk of the children to merely the elements of schooling with accommodation and equipment inferior to that of secondary schools, in classes too large for efficient instruction, under teachers of whom at least one-third are insufficiently trained'. Nor was it satisfied with an arrangement which, despite what was being done through scholarships for exceptional working-class talent, 'still reserves the endowed secondary schools, and even more the universities, for the most part, to the sons and daughters of a small privileged class . . .'. Accordingly, it demanded a systematic reorganization of the whole educational structure 'from the university to the nursery school' on the basis of social equality, to provide every child, youth and adult with the best and most varied education of which he was capable of receiving, supported by a maintenance grant, in institutions which, irrespective of their elementary, secondary or university status, were equipped and staffed to a common high standard.

As a statement of long-term policy demands, this was interesting. For example, while it regretted and attacked the social-class basis of the division between elementary and secondary education, the statement did not demand universal secondary education. It accepted the fact that there would continue to be two qualitatively different levels of State education. At the same time it outlined Labour's ambiguous attitude towards continuation schools. Despite having accepted these schools in the 1918 Act, the Party had come to regard them as fundamentally inadequate as a long-term policy, and dangerous in the sense that their existence might lead people to underestimate the need for further reforms. But, nevertheless, at the same time it felt compelled to accept any form of educational provision and thus to work for their improvement. This was confirmed later in the year by an ACE memo which laid down conditions of operation for such schools upon which the Party should insist in an effort to ensure that even these minimal concessions were not sabotaged by unco-operative industrialists.

During this same period, the ACE was working on another deficiency of the education system, the role of the free place and scholarship systems in the secondary sector. A memo produced in May 1918 revealed how concerned it was with the narrowness of this link between the elementary and secondary systems. It argued that 'the idea of the "educational ladder" is, *by itself*, a very inadequate description of the duty of the State towards, and its interest in the development of education'. In operation it was essentially class-biased, since the inadequacy of the free place and scholarship system and the existence of high fees meant that most working-class children simply could not enter a secondary school. The Annual Report of the Board of Education 1911, which revealed that not more than 5% of elementary pupils ever got secondary education, confirmed, in the Party's view, 'that ability has no opportunity of adequate educational development . . .'

where the secondary system was still primarily adjusted, 'not to the intellectual capacity of children, but to the financial capacity of parents . . .'. And even if an educational ladder was acceptable, in the Party's view it would demand many more scholarships and maintenance allowances to offset the poverty of parents of talented working-class children.

In a way which foreshadowed many contemporary discussions, this memo also provided an interesting response to critics of the Party who argued that its policies of extending educational opportunities would result in a levelling down of education. It was argued that even if the existing arrangements did in fact capture all the existing talent, which it doubted, and a widening of the ladder did threaten the depression of academic standards, it was nevertheless not undesirable, but rather 'highly desirable to "lower the standards of education" if that means to offer education to children to whom it has not been offered hitherto. In that sense nearly all educational progress has taken place by "lowering the standards of education" till it was accessible to classes hitherto excluded from it.' This was an attitude which was implicit then in Party policies and has remained so in the more controversial post-war period. The limits of the Committee's demands, however, were marked by the fact that at this stage it was essentially concerned with improving the ratio of elementary pupils getting into secondary schools rather than with achieving universal secondary education. In 1920 even those Party members most intimately involved in educational reform at least tacitly accepted the immediate situation that secondary education could only be provided for a limited number of children and not the whole child population.

SECONDARY EDUCATION FOR ALL, 1918-44

Recession in education

Nevertheless, Labour's policies were soon shown to advantage by the actions of the Conservative Government. For when the post-war boom collapsed, the Government once more turned for a solution to a huge reduction in public expenditure. Reporting in 1922, the Geddes Committee on National Expenditure argued in favour of drastic economies in all sectors of public spending, but its effect 'was the most devastating in education'. Observing that the education estimates had increased from £14.3m. in 1913-14 to £50.6m. in 1922-3, the Committee argued that the costs of elementary and secondary education had increased 'unreasonably' over these years and had 'far exceeded what the country can at present afford'. It called for restrictions in all areas of spending. Free places were to be limited to 25% of secondary pupils, and fees were to be raised 'substantially' throughout. LEAs were to be asked to make similar economies and teachers were to take a 5% cut in salaries. The age of entry to elementary school was raised to six, and the ratio of teachers to pupils was to be raised to 1 : 50. Free secondary education was not to be reduced, but was to be restricted to the same level, as the Committee felt that parents could afford to pay more, and in any case many of the children were not able to justify the expenditure on them. In all, expenditure on the education service was to be cut from £50m. to £34m.

In fact, the Board had been pursuing a stringent economy programme over the previous two years, having issued circulars postponing all new schemes involving new expenditure except with specific Cabinet approval, restricting more secondary places and maintenance allowances and postponing the development of continuation schools. Generally, the measures led to educational stagnation, and specifically they were to lead to the death of the continuation schools. Their death angered the Labour Party, which, as we have seen, despite its fundamental objections to them, had seen them as a useful temporary expedient and had latterly been urging their usefulness in curbing child unemployment and allaying industrial unrest. But as Taylor has remarked, their death was probably for the good since they probably would have provided 'a strictly proletarian education and so made the class cleavage in education even worse'. Nevertheless, the Labour Party resented the reduction of any educational opportunity, and Conferences in both 1921 and 1922 accepted militant resolutions attacking the Government and calling upon it to provide 'for the mass of workers the provision of the best possible educational facilities'.

'Secondary Education for All'

During this period of depression in education, however, the Party was involved in an event which was ultimately to have far more significance than this temporary financial setback to education. It stemmed from an ACE decision in February 1921 to collate all the information it had thus far collected and to publish documents on the various topics. R. H. Tawney was selected to do the piece on secondary education, and one year later produced his report, *Secondary Education for All*. It was immediately published as a policy statement by the Party. This ended uncertainty about Labour's long-term goals and put its policies on a systematic rather than an *ad hoc* basis. The policy, which was at once both radical and practical, was to be the basis of its educational programme for the next twenty years and practically the foundation of the 1944 Education Act.

Much more than the piecemeal reform with which the Party had so far contented itself, *Secondary Education for*

SECONDARY EDUCATION FOR ALL, 1918-44

All attempted to examine the fundamental relationship between the two parallel, but to a great degree separate, sides of English education, the elementary and secondary, and to link them in a 'vital and systematic' manner. Its theme was that the only policy which was at once 'educationally sound and suited to a democratic community' was one where primary and secondary education were organized in 'a single and continuous process', the latter being the natural successor of the former. Instead of only the cleverest children from the elementary schools going to a secondary school through a free place or scholarship, with the rest of the places bought by wealthy parents, it argued that 'All children, irrespective of income, class or occupation of their parents may be transferred at the age of eleven from the primary or preparatory school to one type or another of secondary school and remain in the latter till sixteen'.

The division of education into elementary and secondary sides, it stressed, was 'educationally unsound and socially obnoxious'. It had resulted in a great waste of talent, the imposition on the primary schools of the task of educating children between twelve and fourteen, for which purpose it was never intended or suited, as well as the exclusion from secondary schools of children who ought to have attended them, and waste and inefficiency arising from overlapping. That division, it argued, should be ended and secondary education seen, not as the privilege of a few, but the right of all children.

The document also went on to define more clearly the Party's attitude to the various forms of post-primary education that had been developing outside the secondary system. For example, while admitting that it had accepted continuation schools in 1918, it argued that they were 'makeshift' schools, avowedly 'elementary in aim technique', and essentially a 'temporary arrangement'. If they were to continue in any form, it should not be to provide continued elementary education because 'part-time continuation schools cannot be accepted by the Labour Movement as a substitute for the programme of secondary education for all . . .'.

Similarly, the central schools and junior technical schools, which in many cities were being used to provide an education beyond the elementary grade, and which the Conservatives were anxious to develop, though possessing certain advantages, were not a satisfactory alternative to secondary education. They were inferior to secondary schools in standards of building, equipment and staff ratio. Their curriculum was semi-vocational and sometimes unduly and prematurely specialized. Teachers did not have comparable qualifications as secondary teachers and their salaries were far inferior. Their leaving age was lower than that of secondary schools, and generally maintenance allowances were not paid. Their great danger was that, while perpetuating an invidious distinction between the principles of elementary and secondary education, 'they may induce public opinion to acquiesce in the provision of secondary school places on a quite inadequate scale, on the ground that, for all but a minority of children, secondary education is neither practicable nor desirable'.

Naturally, it was admitted that such a radical reorganization of the education structure would be realized 'only over a period of years' and that the process could not be 'other than gradual'. Nevertheless, the Party argued that a start on the reforms could be made immediately. For example, the fees at all existing secondary schools should be removed, so that all secondary education was free, even before there was universal secondary education. This was to be achieved by the annual removal of a proportion of fees until all places were free by 1924. Pending this, the number of free places should be increased from 25% to

40%, as the Departmental Committee had recommended. This was particularly important, since in 1919-20 11,234 free place winners had been turned down simply because no places were available. It was to be hoped that by 1932 75% of all pupils between the age of eleven and fifteen would be in secondary schools.

But even universal secondary education, it was argued, was not necessarily enough, since many working-class parents could not afford to forgo their children's wages, even if it were available. This should be overcome by the wide provision of maintenance allowances, which 'must be regarded neither as a charitable concession to exceptional misfortune, nor merely as a bounty paid on the manufacture of teachers, but as an essential element in the creation of a system of higher education which shall be accessible to all members of the community'.

Thus universal, compulsory, free secondary education was the long-term goal of the Party, and 'all immediate reforms should be carried out with that general objective in view and in such a way as to contribute to its attainment'. Nothing less would either withstand the criticism of educationalists, or 'satisfy the demands of a working-class that has tasted the tree of knowledge and does not intend that its children should be fobbed off with the educational shoddy which was foisted upon itself'. But it should be noted at this point for its later significance that the Party at this stage seemed to accept that there would be a variety of secondary schools.

Labour in office, 1923

The Party was soon to have an opportunity to implement some of these proposals. In December 1923 a minority Labour Government found itself 'in office, but not in power'. However, the position of the Government and the state of the economy was such that it was recognized from the start that the Party was not going to create a revolution in education. An ACE memo in February 1924 made the point that a Labour President of the Board of Education would not be able 'to introduce any sweeping innovations', but argued that modest advances should be made, since 'from a political point of view, a progressive educational programme, till recently a liability, has become an asset. The "Geddes Policy" has overstretched itself and produced a reaction.' It argued that the Party would probably have support for sane and enlightened progress in education from an influential body of LEAs and educationalists who would not normally support its policies in other areas. Indeed, there was for the Labour Government, the ACE argued, 'no way in which it can more surely strengthen its hold on "middle opinion", or more clearly demonstrate that it is concerned with the deeper and more permanent interests of the nation than by taking a strong line about education'.

From the start of his period of office, the Labour President, C. P. Trevelyan, attempted to pursue just such a line. He was, however, obliged to operate within severe financial limits, and the majority of his measures consisted only of minor financial relaxations and adjustments to the system. They nevertheless revealed a genuine commitment to a programme of educational reform. His first steps were to withdraw circular 1190, imposed two years earlier, which had so drastically curtailed educational development and at the same time to amend the regulations on the amount of expenditure which should be recognized by the Board. In September the percentage of free places LEAs were allowed to offer was raised from 25% to 40%, and the Minister stated his willingness to consider LEA proposals to abolish all secondary school fees. At the same time the Board offered to pay during the first year of operation £2 for each free place above the minimum offered by LEAs, which would be increased to £3 in succeeding years. The Minister also deferred to Party policy for secondary education by setting a target of the provision of twenty secondary pupils per 1,000 members of the general population, instead of the prevailing norm of ten places per 1,000.

Also LEAs were empowered and encouraged unilaterally to raise the school-leaving age to fifteen within their own areas. On this point, Trevelyan was convinced that 'the principal obstacle in public opinion to the raising of the school age to fifteen is the difficulty which large numbers of parents feel in forgoing the wages which their children begin to earn at fourteen', and as a result the limit of expenditure on maintenance allowances was raised from 6s. to 9s. per week, and the Board offered to reimburse the LEAs for such expenditure at the rate of 50% instead of the previous 20%. Furthermore, an additional allowance of a grant up to 25% was made in respect of LEA expenditure on approved schemes for widening and developing facilities for the social and physical training of young people between fourteen and sixteen and in particular the unemployed.

These general measures were well received by the Labour Party. They represented a welcome advance on the policies of previous Conservative governments dedicated to financial stringencies. They were obviously not, however, the maximum the Party could hope for, and the Minister had to resist a number of demands from backbenchers for further economic liberalization. He would not, for example, admit there should be compulsory continuation education. Nor would he accept the view that maintenance allowances should be paid at an earlier age. Similarly, he would not accept Kirkwood's suggestion that these allowances should be increased to the size of an average salary, nor that from Lansbury that in all cases where LEAs chose to raise the leaving age to fifteen compulsory maintenance allowances should be made universally available during that extra final year, and economic circumstances, he argued, simply would not allow him to implement the most persistent Party demand that the leaving age should be universally raised to fifteen, with the payment of maintenance allowances.

Throughout his nine months of office, Trevelyan thus tried to pursue a policy of gradual expansion, steering a course between the more extreme demands of some of his supporters and the opposition of the Conservatives. And the Party was well satisfied with his record. A publication after it left office claimed the President had done well, in view of the state of education after Geddes when he took over, and in view of the fact that many LEAs had been less co-operative in expanding education than the Board had hoped. Its general conclusion was that the President had 'assured the way to great educational developments by apparently small reforms'. Its high opinion was shared by the *Manchester Guardian*, which argued that his greatest achievement was not the welcome removal of the 'individual cruelties and imbecilities', but his record on the problem of compartmentalization of English education which was 'to drive into the public mind with all the authority of his great office that the day of thinking in closed departments was over and that, although development must necessarily proceed step by step to plan development effectively, it is necessary to plan it as a unity'.

On leaving office, Trevelyan appealed to all parties to keep education out of politics in an attempt to secure a ten-year period of a 'continuous national policy' which would lead to an expansion of all forms of education. The Conservative President accepted this appeal. But even while this artificial truce lasted clear differences were revealed between the parties' attitudes to secondary education. Indeed the Conservatives' first measure on returning to office was to discontinue the special grant Labour had introduced to expand the number of free secondary places. Basically, the Conservative Government retained a very elitist notion of education, subscribing to the concept of an educational ladder as opposed to the 'broad highway' of the Labour Party. Its view was that universal secondary education 'ought not to be the educational ideal to which we should work'. The President himself was constantly preoccupied with preserving the standards of the grammar schools, and on one occasion, in reply to Labour's criticisms of the inadequacies of the 'inferior' central schools, for example, argued that 'the attempt to bring all post-elementary education to one dead high-school level . . . will do more to prevent any real higher education in this country than anything else'. The truce in education was ended by the Conservatives' return to stringent, economic policies in 1925, which dismayed both the Liberal and Labour Parties, and which gave rise to extremely militant demands from the latter. The Annual Conference urged the creation of a specifically working-class education which would develop socialist values, substituting co-operation for competition amongst children and other qualities and outlooks 'essential to a citizen of a co-operative Commonwealth', in the hope that 'a proletarian attitude towards a new outlook on life might be cultivated'. But, of course, such demands, unique in their ferocity, merely served to demonstrate the immediate, if not long-term, impotence of the Party.

The Hadow Report

However, proof that right if not might was on the side of

the Party was soon forthcoming. As Graves has observed, *'Secondary Education for All'*, though it contained the essence of the problem, was only a political manifesto, and 'what was needed to set the educational world ablaze was an educational manifesto . . .'. *The Report of the Consultative Committee on the Education of the Adolescent*, the *Hadow Report*, published in 1926, proved to fill this need. Set up by the Labour Government ten days after it had taken office, it was asked, in accordance with the Party's major concern at this time, to examine the relationship between the elementary and secondary sectors. The Committee accepted virtually all the major proposals for the structure of education that *Secondary Education for All* had made, thus conferring upon them an official legitimacy which they had not hitherto possessed. It accepted the basic premise that secondary education should be not the privilege of wealthy or very talented children, but the natural right of all children, and the natural successor to primary education. It also accepted the Party's proposal that there should be a variety of secondary schools, and that between them there should be parity of status, staff, conditions and equipment. It accepted the need to raise the school-leaving age to fifteen and suggested this should be done by September 1932. And, finally, it should be noted for its later significance that the Committee recognized that it would be some time before there were enough secondary schools for all children, and thus recommended that until there was, as a temporary expedient, LEAs should attempt some reorganization within the elementary schools by providing for junior and senior elementary schools. The *Report* did not, however, deal with the question of fees or maintenance allowances, which were essentially a political as opposed to an educational issue. The *Report* received almost unanimous approval from educationalists.

The Conservative Government claimed to accept the principles of the *Report*, but never seemed prepared to spend money to implement them. For example, it was clearly not anxious to find the money to raise the leaving age to fifteen. And instead of the general reorganization that *Hadow* had recommended, 'a surer and safer policy appealed' to the Conservatives. The Board decided to postpone action on the major recommendations of the *Report* and instead concentrate on the more immediate problem of reorganizing the elementary schools into junior and senior sections, thus confirming the fears expressed in an ACE memo of the danger that 'this very necessary reorganization will be regarded as a permanent alternative to the full programme of secondary education for all, and not merely as a temporary measure designed to meet the needs of the present generation of children'. As if to emphasize the differences between the approaches of the two parties on this crucial matter, Percy was later to claim that this emphasis on elementary reorganization indeed 'had been in a peculiar sense the policy of the present Government'.

The second minority Labour Government

Attacking the Conservatives' interpretation of the priorities of the *Hadow Report*, Trevelyan at the 1927 Conference argued that the proposals outlined in *Secondary Education for All* would be 'the marching orders for a Labour Minister of Education'. His opportunity to prove this came in 1929 with the appointment of the second minority Labour Government, and his own reappointment as President of the Board. In fact, when he took office it was recognized that the single most important measure he could pass as a contribution to long-term Party policy was to raise the school-leaving age from fourteen to fifteen.

SECONDARY EDUCATION FOR ALL, 1918-44

The Party had been advocating this move for a number of years and for a variety of reasons. It had argued, for example, that a year's further education would in humanitarian terms be a value in itself. At the same time, such a move would help to eliminate the disparities of esteem that existed between the different forms of post-primary education. And at this period it was argued to be a valuaable measure in relieving some of the burden of heavy unemployment. Labour's attitude to this measure had always been, in Snowden's words: 'It is poverty not unwillingness which compels parents to take their children away from school at the earliest possible moment that the law will permit.' And on introducing the measure Trevelyan argued that public demand for extended education was not absent, but merely latent, and there was 'no reason to suppose, even if the immediate demand at this moment appears to be rather less because of the higher fees and the strain of the economic situation that the real desire is not there still'.

Educationalists thus looked to the Labour President for a lead on this issue. The *Manchester Guardian* was convinced that if he would raise the leaving age 'the nation would support him in his policy'. From the start, however, it was evident that the President was finding difficulty in getting from the Cabinet the finance for this measure. The omission of any reference to a Bill for raising the leaving age in the King's Speech, for example, led the ACE to send a delegation to Trevelyan immediately urging the case for action. Eventually, however, after some delay, a Bill was introduced in 1930. But while this satisfied Party demands for the leaving age to be raised, it angered a number of members on a related issue, the provision of maintenance allowances. For although, in accordance with Party policy, these were to be paid, the rates of payment would be 'related to the actual needs of the children and their parents'. In other words, there was to be a means test. Further than this, the Board was only prepared to reimburse LEA expenditure at the rate of 60% if the allowances were less than 5s. a week, nor would they be payable to children under the age of fourteen, as Trevelyan had claimed they would be at the 1927 Conference.

In fact, pressure against a means test had been building up within the Party before the Bill was published. As one Member pointed out, the classic deficiency of the means test would reveal itself: either the limit would be so high as to make any saving negligible or so low as to cause hardship and demoralization. Indeed, the speaker continued, there was no need for a means test, 'because the very fact that a parent has a child at elementary school implies a means test. The well-to-do do not send their children to elementary schools. . . .' Trevelyan was, however, unable to give way to such demands, and growing opposition to the Bill within the Party threatened to ruin it. In fact, the Bill had to be withdrawn eventually because of the difficulties over the question of financial aid to religious schools if the leaving age was raised. But it was reintroduced later in the year with a religious settlement, though in all else the same. Trevelyan remained as adamant as before on the issue of allowances. 'There are,' he claimed, 'many other things in education which I believe are far more worth spending money upon than giving these maintenance allowances to families where any very great need does not exist.' However, a speech by the President's Parliamentary Private Secretary, Morgan Jones, at the 1930 Conference revealed that the President was probably trying to put on as brave a front as possible on a case that he was personally not happy with. He admitted that, in fact, if the money was available, there would be 'an overwhelming case' for dropping the means test, but that the Board simply could not afford it. But he still made the point that the situation was not too bad, since 'the vast majority of working-class people, of people with the lowest incomes, would come under the aegis of the new Bill . . .'. Nevertheless, a Conference resolution regretting the inclusion of a means test, though finally defeated, received a large measure of support. At the same time, the ACE passed a similarly extremely critical resolution. And a few weeks later, after the Bill had expired for lack of Parliamentary time and a new one was being drawn up, a meeting of the Parliamentary Party, despite a defence of the issue by Snowden, the Chancellor of the Exchequer, rejected the principle of the means test with only two Members voting with the President and the rest against him.

A third Bill was introduced in November 1930 with the troublesome religious settlement dropped, the Government being determined at least to raise the leaving age, in spite of the opposition of the voluntary schools. This showed that the pressure of the Party rank and file had forced Trevelyan and the Cabinet to adopt a more liberal approach to the issue of maintenance allowances. The limits of payment were raised and the means-test principle at least partially abandoned, with a new flat-rate grant being introduced, resting on a broad distinction between those who were in need and those who were not, rather than on a detailed investigation of family income with a graded scale of allowances. These concessions appeared to draw the sting of the President's critics, and the debate was confined to a discussion of the positive advantages of the Bill, which Trevelyan called 'the charter of the average child'. It finally received a Third Reading, though not before a Catholic Labour MP, Scurr, got accepted an amendment providing that the Bill should not come into general operation until money had been given to the voluntary schools for the reorganization, which MacDonald claimed meant that the Bill would be 'knocked to smithereens'. But in the event it did not matter, since the Bill was rejected by a hostile House of Lords. The Labour Government did not have time to introduce another, and its failure brought the resignation of Trevelyan.

The achievements of the second Labour Government would have obviously been greater if the Education Bill had been passed. Without it, its achievements appear modest in relation to the overall goal of universal secondary education. But, put into the context of the gravest financial crisis the country had ever faced, the Government did pursue a number of changes, mainly financial relaxations of a minor character, which were laudable. For example, the quota of free places LEAs could offer was raised from 40% to 50%, just as the first Labour Government had raised it from 25% to 40%. The limit of 9s. on maintenance allowances was removed. And a special grant was implemented and paid for three years, whereby the grant of 20% was raised to 50% on capital expenditure by LEAs designed to help raise the leaving age. And if Trevelyan was not able to offer much in the way of maintenance allowances, it must be recalled that the Conservative Party regarded them essentially as 'doles', and the principle of granting them for compulsory as opposed to voluntary education was regarded as wholly unacceptable. Finally, the Government had precipitated the reorganization of elementary and secondary education as *Hadow* had recommended, and was later to claim that it had 'infused energy and new meaning into the movement in that direction'.

Retrenchment again

But once more Labour's policies were shown to advantage by those of its successor, the National Government. Facing a national economic crisis, the new Government clutched at the idea of public economy and created a Select Committee on National Expenditure, just as the Conservative Government had done ten years earlier. And the result was as disastrous for education. A *Report* 'compounded of prejudice, ignorance and panic' advocated swingeing cuts in educational expenditure which led once more to general stagnation. The *Report* was implemented through a series of Board Circulars in 1931 and 1932. Once again the children of working-class parents suffered most under 'the heaviest blow served at the national system since 1900'. This was particularly true, since the Committee, arguing in an overtly class-biased way which particularly incensed the Labour Party, recommended that 'since the standard of education, elementary and secondary, that is being given to the child of poor parents is already in very many cases superior to that which the middle-class parent is providing for his own child', the Government should make changes in the basis of the free place system, the only real means of working-class entry into secondary education, and compel the winners of them still to pay fees, if at a reduced rate. This was done with the introduction of a special place to replace the free place system in 1932.

Labour reaction to this 'unashamed, naked class war' was predictably vitriolic. It constituted, Morgan Jones argued, an attack on 'those least able to look after themselves' and 'a challenge to the whole philosophy of the movement to which I belong'. The policy, which was a waste of talent rather than a genuine economy, meant that to acquire an English secondary education working-class children had to be 'exceptionally clever and exceptionally poor'. The Conservative Government, however, took the line that secondary education ought to be selective anyway, and that these measures served as a convenient instrument of selection. Indeed, as late as 1933, Ramsbottom, Parliamentary Secretary to the Board, could argue that 'to throw secondary education open to all and sundry would very likely be the reverse of an educational advance and might easily be an educational regression; we might easily turn the nation into something like an educational soup-kitchen'. But again Labour's response merely served to demonstrate its weakness in the immediate situation. They had to be content to propagandize their now-familiar policies in the hope of getting a basically hostile Board to make some minor concessions, such as the restoration of the free place system or a more rapid reorganization of elementary schools. But it could not hope to achieve very much in the way of universal secondary education while the President of the Board still believed that the role of the secondary system was to act as 'a lift or stairway to the higher storeys of the social structure'.

The 1936 Education Act

But by 1936 the general pressure on the National Government had told, and it felt bound to honour its election pledge and raise the school-leaving age to fifteen. The controversial aspect of the Bill, however, was that, despite the fact that it was seven years since the minority Labour Government had attempted to raise the leaving age universally, this Bill returned to pre-1918 practice of making it possible for children to be exempted from the intended extra year of education if they could prove that they could take up 'beneficial employment'. Also its implementation was to be delayed for three years and maintenance allowances were not to be paid. The President of the Board, Oliver Stanley, argued that this optional extra year could be used to convince parents of the value of extended education, which they still doubted at this time. But the tone of his defence reflected a continuous strand of Conservative thought that voluntary was in some sense superior to compulsory education, and also indicated a further Conservative concern that the education system should to a large extent be viewed as serving the industrial sector of society and that purely educational considerations ought not to be allowed to disturb that arrangement.

The Labour Party regarded the Bill as totally inadequate and class-biased, and argued that the number of exemptions, which it had been independently calculated might reach the figure of 85%, meant the Bill would be 'rendered substantially inoperative'. Further, it would be a denial of the *Hadow* recommendations, since it failed to guarantee that all senior schools for children over the age of fifteen would be upgraded to the status of secondary schools, and it also made the final year of education, the most important one in the *Hadow* scheme, the least important. Finally, the Party argued that the refusal to pay maintenance allowances was a deliberate attack on the poor, since the rich already received a concealed grant for this purpose from the State by obtaining income-tax relief for expenditure on education. But, despite the Party's protests and those of a majority of educationalists, the Bill was passed on the basis of exemptions and no maintenance allowances. Fortunately, however, the outbreak of war in 1939 prevented the Act from being put into practice, and the path was left clear for a more radical and comprehensive reform of the education system in 1944.

SECONDARY EDUCATION FOR ALL, 1918-44

The development of multilateralism

After 1936 the Party was able to become more concerned with other aspects of its policy of universal secondary education. It is clear that after this date it became increasingly concerned both about the failure of elementary reorganization to lead to an extension of secondary education and the problem of the disparities of conditions and status that were being associated with the different types of reorganized schools. And this in turn led it to pay attention to the possibilities of a common secondary or multilateral school in eliminating these kinds of problems. The idea of such a school which could provide an education for a variety of different children under one roof had been propagated during the 1920s and 1930s by a number of educationalists. But it ran very much counter to the official philosophy in this period. The three major reports on English education in the inter-war period, the *Hadow*, *Spens* and *Norwood Reports*, all stressed the need for a variety of schools which would cater for the educational needs of different children in different institutions, as had, of course, the Party's own programme contained in *Secondary Education for All*. In fact, a memo. to the ACE in 1925 had urged the Party to consider the introduction of a multiple-bias school which would contain all sorts of education and prevent 'the classification of secondary schools as superior to others in type, which would perpetuate class differences and which would prevent any real unity of outlook in secondary education'. But this had come to nothing. In 1925 the idea had little or no support in the Party.

In 1937, however, Morgan Jones remarked to Parliament that 'if we were starting *de novo*, I should stand, in the bigger areas, for the multiple bias school, to which all the eleven-plus children should go'. One year later he made the same argument, but admitted: 'it is late to do it, and it might be almost impossible as the problem may have become almost insuperable by now'. Nevertheless, despite these difficulties, the Party, pointing out that the abolition of fees and a new common code of regulations governing all post-primary education would permit their development for the first time, in 1938 formally adopted a policy of selective development of multilateral schools. It was seen, however, essentially as one type of possible solution. At this time, the Party did not advocate their universal development.

The newly reconstructed ACE soon took up the cause of the multilateral school and confirmed its approval of the idea to the NEC in June 1939. In the same year it prepared a memo. for the London Labour Party, advising it on a course of policy, in view of that Party's Conference pledge in 1939 to introduce a unified system of multilateral schools. The real problem, it was felt, would be the introduction of the measure of LEAs under a hostile Conservative Government, since it was assumed that 'Probably under a Labour Government the system of multilateral schools will be nationally introduced under the impetus of an Act of Parliament or Board circular . . .'. But, despite the problems involved, it recommended the implementation of multilateral reorganization in London 'to anticipate the introduction of the multilateral school under a Labour Government . . . since from the electoral point of view the balance to be weighed is the amount of that increase [in expenditure] against the additional support likely to be attracted to the Party by the open and unashamed adoption of the policy of equality of opportunity for every child of every parent-voter'.

Not all members of the ACE, however, were equally convinced of the merits of the multilateral school. A memo. in April 1942, for example, observed that within the Committee itself 'there is a wide division of opinion as to what is meant by *Secondary Education For All* . . .'. Probably the basis of their dilemma can be seen in a memo. submitted by an individual member in the same year which argued that if the reorganization of secondary education failed to challenge the power and status of the grammar school, 'then we may have to try the multilateral school, but I should still feel we were sacrificing educational to social considerations. I think it may be necessary to do so, but I think we should recognize what we are doing'.

The 1944 Education Act

However, this question of the role of the multilateral school was to remain unresolved at this time, although it was to become a crucial issue for the Labour Government. Despite the Conference call in 1942 for the development of comprehensive schools, the issue was dwarfed by the most important event of this period, the passing of the 1944 Education Act.

The real achievement of the Party in this period was the passage of this Act under a coalition government. As in 1917-18, a major war gave point to the rising pressures for educational reform as part of the social reconstruction that was to be undertaken at the end of the war. And it was in the 1944 reorganization that the Party's policy of *Secondary Education for All* received its final vindication. Almost every major demand that the Party had made for the State educational system was accommodated within this Act. It recognized that all children over the age of eleven should be transferred from an elementary to a secondary school and that all secondary schools should be under a common code of regulations governing staff, equipment and physical conditions which, hopefully, would lead to parity of esteem. The leaving age was raised to fifteen immediately and provision made for its raising to sixteen. The principle of exemption from secondary education was finally abandoned, the Act being universal. Finally, fees in all State-maintained schools, save some direct-grant schools, were abolished. The principle of maintenance allowances for children between fourteen and fifteen years was not, however, accepted. Nevertheless, the Party was well satisfied with the Act. The only opposition it offered, and that was not very vigorous, was over the failure to deal with fee-paying in direct-grant schools and the failure to place a definite date for raising the leaving age to sixteen. The question of maintenance allowances was rarely mentioned and the case for the multilateral school received no more than passing reference from a few Labour MPs. The Party accepted the Act as the most radical innovation in the history of educational legislation and promised to assist the Minister in his struggle against recalcitrant local authorities, sectarian interests, or 'in any fight he may have against the forces of snobbery or class consciousness which may try to limit these proposals on the ground that education should be restricted to the needs of the few'. The Act was posed as the victory for the common child.

The contribution to the development of English education in this period was a major one. It rests not so much on what it achieved while actually in office, for, as we have seen, that in direct terms was rather limited. Rather, its contribution lay in developing and publicizing certain ideas about how English education ought to be structured and the role it ought to play in society. It was the first political group to formulate a coherent policy on the democratic principle of equal opportunity for all children regardless of intellectual or social background, and was the only one to pursue consistently and publicly that policy both in and out of office. The Party thus formed the spearhead for educational advance in this inter-war period and helped achieve the conversion of a traditionally hostile Conservative Party to the enlightened principle of universal secondary education. Its role as propagandist clearly cannot be precisely gauged, but it must not be underestimated. In 1918 English secondary education was wholly elitist, narrowly selective in both social and intellectual terms. In 1944 it appeared to be wholly democratized, catering for all talents and all classes. Therein lies the achievement of the Labour Party.

3
The Labour Government, 1945-51

The prospects for reform

In many ways the 1944 Education Act was for the Party the consummation of a generation's work and ambition. The provision of universal secondary education to the age of sixteen, the abolition of fees in State-maintained schools and the end of the distinction between elementary and secondary education fulfilled and justified the Party's traditional aspirations in the field of education. But the Act, while resolving one controversy, at the same time give rise to another. Whereas the principle of universal secondary education was now admitted, the issue of the administrative structure within which it should be provided was still to be settled. This was to be the most controversial feature of the Labour Government's administration.

In fact, by 1944 the direction in which the secondary system was developing had become fairly clear, as the official reports reveal. The Hadow Committee in 1926 had reported in favour of a bilateral structure for the secondary system, consisting of grammar and modern schools. The Spens Committee in 1938 developed this notion and advocated its extension to a tripartite system, with the technical school as its third element. The White Paper on Educational Reconstruction in 1943 accepted

THE LABOUR GOVERNMENT, 1945-51

these recommendations, proposing 'three main types of secondary schools to be known as grammar, modern and technical schools'. Ten days later the Norwood Committee of the Secondary School Examination Council reported and suggested that there indeed existed three types of pupil corresponding to the proposed tripartite division of secondary schools, and thereby, despite the adverse criticism of a number of educationists and psychologists, 'transformed tripartitism from a proposal into a doctrine'. The Act itself, for which these various documents had in a sense served as a basis of discussion, did not in fact stipulate tripartite division, but its implications were clear. The Board favoured the development of three kinds of secondary school, each with its distinctive aims and character, to accommodate three qualitatively different types of children. This official emphasis on the need for a division of the secondary education structure contrasted strongly with the alternative approach known as 'multilateralism' (or 'comprehensive education') to which we have seen the Labour Party becoming increasingly attached in the years preceding the passage of the 1944 Act.

In 1945 the Party again came to office. The prospects for radical change in education were propitious for two reasons. It was the first time the Party had had an absolute majority in Parliament, and at the same time the education structure was already undergoing a major structural transformation, and was thus sensitive to the needs for change. A memo. submitted to the ACE in 1942, it will be recalled, had argued that this would obviously be the most favourable situation for multilateral reorganization. But at the same time this process of change in secondary education was creating obstacles to the development of a multilateral system. The purpose of this chapter is to see how Labour reacted to office and how it coped with the problem of implementing its policy of secondary education for all, which had more recently been overlaid with demands for multilateral reorganization.

Tripartitism and Party dissent

In fact, the seeds of dissent had already been sown by the time Labour came to office. The Conservative caretaker Government in 1945 published a policy statement, *The Nation's Schools*, which claimed to lay down the official direction of development of the secondary sector. In tone and intention it constituted an affront to Labour's policy of multilateralism. The document argued that there was already a *de facto* tripartite system in operation, and indeed approved a system whereby the needs of different children could be met within different institutions. It thus accepted the Norwood Committee's views on this issue, and also its explicit criticisms of multilateral schools. And the fact that the system was already undergoing radical change, far from suggesting to the Ministry, as it had to the Labour Party, that the time was ripe for multilateral reorganization, in their view 'limited the extent to which new groupings and combinations are possible'. The Ministry in fact accepted the conventional wisdom that, as 'past experience' had demonstrated, schools with limited and well-defined aims and selective intake were the most likely to succeed in reaching and maintaining the highest educational standards. Thus, while accepting the need for experiment and enterprise, the document argued against a 'revolutionary change' which would offer clear losses and only doubtful gains.

Such a conclusion alone, if endorsed by a Labour Minister, would seem calculated to offend the Party. But at the same time it reached a further conclusion which, though not as significant in the long run, created many immediate problems for the Party. It concerned the provision of grammar-school places. At this point it should be recalled that one element in the theory of secondary education for all had been the idea that working-class children should have the same opportunity to attend grammar schools as had the middle-class children. The 1944 Act appeared to promise this. *The Nation's Schools*, however, reached a conclusion that seemed to deny them this opportunity. In the first case, it argued that since in 1938 40% of secondary-school leavers had not taken the School Certificate and 25% had left before the age of sixteen, many children had obviously been getting an education beyond their capacities, in which case there would be no need to expand the provision of grammar-school places beyond the pre-war limit, but that in some cases the figure could actually be reduced. More than this, it stressed that this high demand for grammar-school places and the subsequent entry of many children into black-coated jobs had meant that industry had been 'deprived of its reasonable share' of talent and that the country had thereby suffered, and it advocated a limit of grammar-school places on these grounds. To the Labour Party this inevitably implied a return to the detested pre-war notion of vocational education for the working-classes, aimed at providing a stream of low-skilled workers for industry, a policy which it was bound to oppose.

However, although the Labour Ministry had not published the original document, on taking office in 1945 it continued to accept responsibility for its publication. The predictable clash came at the 1946 Conference. An amendment moved by a member of the National Association of Labour Teachers, Cove, urged the Minister, in view of the fact that many LEAs would base their development plans on this pamphlet, to repudiate the document and reshape the education system 'in accordance with Socialist principles', which meant multilateral reorganization.

The speakers in favour of the amendment made clear the Party's objection to the pamphlet, but at the same time revealed a degree of confusion in their own minds. They first attacked the principle of tripartitism which the pamphlet espoused, because it conflicted with the policy of multilateralism which the Party had officially adopted in the late 1930s. At the same time, however, the Minister's critics attacked the policy of limiting the number of grammar-school places that would be made available in the post-war period. In both cases the delegates were motivated by the fear that the children of the working classes would be deprived of their legitimate educational opportunities, but they failed to realize that there was a conflict between the ideas of multilateral and grammar-school education. At this stage the reformers had not clarified in their own minds the relationship between the concept of secondary education for all and the rather different one of a grammar-school education for all.

Despite this attack, however, the new Labour Minister, Ellen Wilkinson, remained firm in her attachment to tripartitism. She placed her faith in parity of material conditions between the different schools leading to parity of esteem. Her view was that a common code of regulations governing staff, buildings, equipment and salaries would necessarily create equality between the schools. The distinctions between schools would be made on the basis of objective, rational educational criteria and not, as previously had been the case, on indefensible and irrelevant social criteria, and were thus justifiable. The education each school would offer would be designed to meet the educational needs of different children, and in no case would an inferior, vocational education be offered to any group of children. This was the argument she presented to the Conference.

Even after she had finished speaking and the NEC spokesman had tried to calm her critics by suggesting that the wording of the pamphlet had been unfortunate, but that it no longer mattered, since it had been withdrawn, the Minister returned to deny this. She argued that while some sections would be rewritten, this did not constitute withdrawal of the pamphlet, since this would imply a repudiation of the 1944 Act on which the pamphlet was based. As a consequence, the amendment was carried by the Conference and the NEC was defeated, one of the only five occasions on which this happened in six years of office. The Party had thus given a clear indication of the policy it expected from the Government in education.

But the strictures of the Conference did not deter the Minister. A few days later, while addressing the Association of Education Committees, she argued that her policy statement had not been wrong, but merely ambiguous. And while she admitted the validity of some Party members and fears about tripartitism, she once more went a long way to justify its continuance. Her critics maintained their attack in Parliament, although revealing in many ways that they still did not appreciate the inherent conflict between demands for multilateral schools and demands for increased grammar-school provision.

The Ministry and grammar schools

But little criticism seemed to affect the Ministry. A series of circulars produced during this period confirmed that its real concern was to maintain the separateness, distinctiveness and elitism of the grammar schools. While circulars stressed the need to protect the other elements in the tripartite partnership in any intended changes or mergers, there can be no doubt that its real concern was for the interests of the grammar schools. Indeed, it was so pessimistic about the prospects of success for multilateral schools that it argued that such schools should be so built that they could be dismantled and separated into distinct sides 'if occasion arises'. In no sense could it be said that the Labour Ministry was encouraging LEAs to develop these schools while holding this sort of threat over their heads. But the Ministry remained adamant that it would not impose a uniform administrative pattern. The Minister herself never advanced beyond a position of allowing cautious experiment. Her final position on the issue was: 'I welcome experiments of this kind. I do not, however, wish to dogmatize about the form in which secondary education should be organized at the outset of the great experiment of educating all children according to their ability and aptitude.'

Continuity under the new Minister

Ellen Wilkinson died in 1947 and was succeeded by George Tomlinson, the previous Minister of Works. His first contribution to the debate was *The New Secondary Education*, prepared while his predecessor was in office, but which was generally to define his position. His acceptance of it clearly indicated that the Party could expect little change from him on the multilateral issue. *The New Secondary Education* was essentially a classic apologia for tripartitism, but in parts gave the illusion that alternative policies might be legitimate. It thus talked in terms of the need to avoid stereotyping and exaggerating differences between what were essentially common schools providing similar educations.

But to some Party members these minor theoretical concessions were bound to appear as a placebo offered in lieu of fundamental changes by the Ministry, and the new Minister was certain to be associated with such an approach. And this was indeed the interpretation placed upon the policy by the 1947 Conference. There the new Minister was warned to avoid perpetuating the undemocratic, class basis of English secondary education and was criticized, not for actively discouraging the growth of multilateral schools, but for being too negative in his approach and failing to encourage LEAs to develop them. This was an attitude generally shared by the NEC spokesman, Alice Bacon, who argued that multilateral schools would probably grow to pre-eminence anyway, and should therefore be encouraged even if they ought not to be enforced on unwilling authorities who might be prepared to sabotage them. But proof that the Minister did not share this point of view of the NEC was provided by the publication of a new circular, which, while making the customary courtesy nod in the direction of multilateral schools, was again concerned that any new plans would ensure that 'the best existing standards will be maintained and indeed raised', i.e. that the interests of the grammar schools would be protected.

Internal confusion and criticism intensified

During this period in 1947 the Party as a whole found itself increasingly uncertain of its plans for secondary education. Whereas in the early 1940s the main stimulus for the comprehensive school had come from a fairly narrow front within the Party spearheaded by the NALT, the later years of office showed more and more Members making public commitments to the comprehensive principle. This made the general position of the policy-makers and the Minister increasingly difficult. One example of this uncertainty was a pamphlet published in 1947 which was designed to promote discussion within the Party in an attempt to discover in which directions allegiances lay and to aid the development of a consistent and acceptable policy. In draft, the document appeared to be in favour of tripartitism. While welcoming experiments by LEAs, it insisted that 'only educational and not social criteria are applied', and it further accepted the need for a limit on grammar-school places and stressed the need to convince parents that 'it is as educationally wrong to send a non-academic child to grammar school as it is to deprive a brilliant child of its opportunities because of its parents' financial circumstances'. Fundamentally, its point was that the tripartite structure should be improved and reformed. But it is indicative of the ambivalence of the Party policy-makers that, when published, even as a document intended to promote discussion, these sentiments were absent and a wholly neutral case was presented.

The Minister himself also continued to play what he considered a neutral role in this dialogue, which in reality meant he became a powerful bulwark against change. On one occasion he claimed, 'I think I can say I have not taken any steps to put forward a certain type—comprehensive, technical or any other schools.' He had merely asked LEAs to submit development schemes that were in the best interests of education in their area. The implication was, of course, that, unlike many of his Party colleagues, he did not think that comprehensive schools were in the best interests of education in the majority of places.

At the 1948 Conference resolutions calling for a more positive approach to the question of reorganization on the part of the Minister were put and carried with the approval of the NEC. And the 1950 Conference similarly delivered the now customary censure of the Minister. And this dissatisfaction was equally evident in private. A report from the Policy Committee in 1949 recognized the extent of the problem, and outlined the case for the Minister's critics, who, it was pointed out, did have enough support to carry successive conferences.

The NALT was later in the year to spell out its objections to the Minister's record and the basis of its opposition. Its case was that, despite the publicly recorded Labour Party decisions, the Ministry had in fact sabotaged the comprehensive school by basing its policy on the assumption that the prevailing organization for secondary education would be the tripartite structure. On no public occasion, it was argued, had the Minister shown himself 'even dimly aware of the feeling in the Labour Party'. In principle, the Association had three major concerns. The first was the general policy of a Labour-controlled Ministry to favour tripartitism. The second was the Minister's desire to encourage a variety of organization for variety-encouraged tripartitism. And their final concern was the absence of direct public encouragement on the part of the Minister for the policy of his own Party. Later the Association was to make the point that the Minister's rejection in 1948 of the Middlesex development plan for comprehensive organization had brought its opposition to the Minister to a climax. His letter to that authority, which observed that the tripartite system was 'logical and usual', had been bad enough in itself, but far worse in their view was its probable consequences of deterring other Labour-controlled LEAs from developing comprehensive education.

The Minister fails to convince his critics

Because of these and other criticisms, the Minister felt obliged to defend his policy in a memo. to the Home Policy Committee in July 1950. In it he reaffirmed his policy which had been expounded in his circulars, but stressed that his rejection of LEA comprehensive development plans had only been in cases where 'I did not consider that those particular proposals were consistent enough with sound educational principles'. On the other hand, he did not personally accept the argument that tripartitism itself was necessarily pernicious. This would only be the case, he felt, if it created a permanent segregation of manual and white-collar workers, and if the secondary modern schools wrongly educated an overwhelming number of misfits. In neither case did he think this was true. At the same time he expressed fears for the future of bright children in any reorganization, for while he agreed that it would be wrong to subordinate all other needs to theirs, he believed 'it would be foolish to ignore the consequences of neglecting those needs'. His conclusion was that for those reasons and the other traditional deficiencies of comprehensives which he outlined, it would be best for a Minister to encourage limited experiment only.

A final justification he made for his policy was that, 'because comprehensive schools are still the subject of violent controversy in educational circles [they] would alienate a large vocal and influential section of opinion'. This sort of reference to the electoral implications of different sorts of policies was in fact quite a rare feature of the debate which took place in these years, but it was a theme which was returned to later by the committee set up by the NEC to review its comprehensive policy. Calling on the Minister to pursue a more liberal policy on this topic, it observed: 'It is important that the Party should realize the electoral value of a constructive education policy which will convince parents that their children are being given a fair start in life.' But its real conclusion, which was to form the basis of a new Party document, was that 'the tripartite system of education does not provide equality of opportunity and is therefore out of tune with the needs of the day and the aspirations of socialism'. It recommended comprehensive reorganization.

An explanation of the controversy

It was clear from this point on that the official Ministerial policy of tripartitism was to be rejected by the Party. On receiving the memo., however, the Minister remained unrepentant, rejecting the criticisms of his behaviour and policies and warning that 'the Party are kidding themselves if they think that the comprehensive idea has any popular appeal'. But nothing more was to be achieved during this period. In a few months the Party was to lose the election and leave office. The question of comprehensive education was still to be resolved.

At the end of this period one is obviously left with the task of explaining the persistent refusals of both Labour Ministers to accede to increasingly vociferous Party demands for the rapid implementation of comprehensive education. An explanation can probably best be attempted in terms of three main factors: the Party's ambivalent attitude towards secondary education for all, in particular the role of the grammar schools; the prevalent notion of what constituted 'intelligence' and how it could best be catered for within the secondary system; and, finally, the administrative problems faced by the Ministry and LEAs in the immediate post-war period.

The confusion about the implications of secondary education for all

In the first case, it is apparent that in the post-1944 period there existed a degree of confusion within the

Labour Party about the implications of a policy of secondary education for all. This had originally been formulated in the pre-war period when the grammar school was the principal kind of school providing a secondary education. And the grammar school had implicitly become the Party's model for the development of secondary education, despite its explicit acceptance of the need to provide a variety of secondary schools. At the same time the grammar school had played an important practical role as the main avenue of occupational and social mobility for working-class children. And for both these reasons many Party members were emotionally attached to them. But the fact that the Party's attachment to these schools was implicit rather than explicit meant that an important point remained concealed until after the passage of the 1944 Education Act. This was the question of whether all children should in fact attend a grammar school, whether, indeed, secondary education for all really meant grammar-school education for all. The Party was convinced that all children were capable of benefiting from secondary education, but never made it clear before 1944 what proportion it felt could benefit from an academic secondary education. And this uncertainty became quite clear during the period of Labour office, when universal secondary education was guaranteed and the real issue became the relative proportions of children who would receive different kinds of secondary education.

The idea of common, unsegregated secondary education introduced another confusing element into the situation. The Party's adoption of this principle on the one hand meant that it did not really accept, as its policy after 1922 had presupposed, that parity of conditions for a variety of different secondary schools would guarantee parity of social status for them and their pupils, and it wanted to avoid any of these problems of disparity of esteem. But at the same time the development of this kind of school, if pursued by the Party, would pose a serious threat to the existence of the grammar schools, which the Party had fought to provide for the children of the working classes. While this had been an academic point in the pre-1944 situation, it became an intensely practical one while Labour was in office.

The result of these previous concealed confusions meant that when the Party came to office it was cross-pressured to act in a variety of different ways. As we have seen, the Ministers' critics at first accused them of both restricting the supply of grammar-school places, and hence limiting the prospects of working-class children entering them, and yet at the same time of not developing the multilateral school, which were essentially mutually contradictory policies. The Ministers, however, defended the grammar schools, one suspects, partly because of the natural conservatism of the Ministry, but also because they appeared to offer working-class children the best education. And for some Party members to ask them to give up these schools appeared to be surrendering the fruits of their victory with the taste still fresh in their mouths. These contradictions were all present in the Party's behaviour during this period. The longer the Ministry went on, and the more Party members who decided that multilateral schools were preferable to tripartitism in terms of the opportunities offered to the working classes, the nearer the issue came to resolution. But the confusion remained great enough to cause problems through all the years of the Labour Government.

The educational basis of tripartitism

The second barrier against change at this time was concerned with the education basis of the tripartite division.

If the force of tradition was not necessarily sufficient to keep the Ministry attached to the idea of tripartitism, the evidence of contemporary psychology certainly ensured it. We have seen that all the inter-war official reports accepted the idea that there should be a variety of secondary schools catering for different types of pupil. The Norwood Committee, for example, observed that, 'Our point is that rough groupings [into three types of school], whatever may be their ground, have in fact established themselves in general educational experience, and the recognition of such groupings in educational practice have been justified both during the period of education and in the after-career of the pupils'. The psychological basis of these assumptions are probably best explained in the *Spens Report* itself. It argued that whereas traditional psychology had assumed that 'most boys and girls were equipped with the same natural endowments, that most of them developed in much the same way and at almost the same rate of progress, and that all learned but the same methods', contemporary theories would stress 'individual differences in interests, abilities and rates of development'. Intellectual development in childhood was supposed to be governed by a single central factor, known as 'general intelligence', and their important conclusion in this respect was that 'the most notable feature of the period after the age of eleven in the intellectual side is the retardation and ultimate arrest in the development of general intelligence'. This was the rock upon which tripartitism was founded, for it meant 'that, with few exceptions, it is possible at a very early age to predict with some degree of accuracy the ultimate level of a child's intellectual powers'. And the implication of this conclusion was that at the age of eleven it was possible to select with a high degree of certainty those pupils who certainly had 'so much intelligence and intelligence of such a character that without doubt they ought to receive a secondary education of a grammar-school type, and also those pupils who quite certainly would benefit from such an education'.

This theory thus provided the educational elitists the perfect weapon with which to attack the advocates of multilateral schools. The comprehensive school could be argued to be at best superfluous and at worst educationally retrograde. That these assumptions in many ways have since been rejected by educational psychologists does not alter their importance as one of the conditioning factors operating upon administrators and the Ministers at this time. They clearly formed part of the climate of opinion by which the Ministers were consciously or unconsciously influenced into accepting the validity of the tripartite system and rejecting the comprehensive alternative. And these factors were bound to appear more important at the time than the apparently ideological considerations of Party members.

The administrative problems

The third set of factors which clearly influenced the Ministry and the Ministers during this period was the administrative problems it faced in this post-war period. This had three elements. In the first case the Ministry worked on the assumption that to be viable the comprehensive schools would have to contain as many as from 1,500 to 1,700 pupils. Their main fear in this situation was that sheer size would destroy the principal acknowledged virtue of comprehensive schools, the creation of a community spirit. In retrospect, these figures do not seem unusually large, and one may be inclined to think the Ministry's attitude disingenuous. But it is revealing to look at the average size of State schools in 1947. At that time the average size of a secondary modern school was 250 and that of a grammar school 410. The projected comprehensives would thus be at least five times as large as any school in existence. And, given the existing doubts about comprehensives, one can appreciate it would be asking a lot of administrators to contemplate a massive reorganization without expressing fears. The second administrative concern was that at this time there existed 3,019 secondary moderns and 1,207 grammar schools in the State sector. One can again appreciate the pressures operating upon administrators to resist theoretical demands for wholesale reorganization which would involve changing all of these in both status and function in an attempt to capture benefits that might prove wholly illusory.

A third administrative problem faced by the Ministry at this time was the general condition of the education structure immediately after a catastrophic war, already in a phase of quite radical change under the terms of the 1944 Act: 5,000 schools had been damaged during the war, without those affected by dilapidation due to war use and the arrears of normal repairs which had accumulated during the war. It was difficult to remedy this situation, since there was a continued shortage of labour and materials, due to the claims of the housing and industrial building programmes. As a side-effect of the war, the birth-rate was rising rapidly and promised to introduce by 1952 800,000 children of school-leaving age more than there were in 1946. The raising of the leaving age promised to add 400,000 more children in 1948 to the previous year's total. And, finally, the 146 LEAs were already in the process of submitting development plans to the Ministry for the reorganization of primary and secondary education on the tripartite basis. Whether one accepts their view or not, it can be easily seen how an administration could make these facts a legitimate reason for not wanting to accept any further plans for disrupting the pattern of the secondary system. Indeed, it could probably be argued that the whole process of education during this period was an administrative matter. Tomlinson, Minister for most of the period, had previously been Minister of Works, and once admitted to Parliament: 'I have never been able to succeed in this chamber in making a speech on education. I hope some day to have the opportunity to do so.' It is certainly clear that a combination of all these factors helped the Ministers to resist Party demands for comprehensive education and explains why the Party managed to achieve so little that was positive on this issue.

The period 1945-51 was, then, for the Party one of instability and uncertainty. It witnessed a conflict between different sections of the Party pressing for different goals, which appeared to be eventually resolved when ideological or strictly educational considerations became more important than purely administrative concerns. The Minister's critics finally triumphed and Party policy after a period of confusion appeared to be once more united. As it left office, the Party clearly had the foundations of an agreed policy, despite the confusion that was bound to persist. Their problem would be in Opposition to consolidate it internally and at the same time present it to the electorate.

4
Selection and segregation in English secondary education

'Educational policy, like all social policy,' David Glass has written, 'is rarely single minded. To understand the final compromise of policy means tracing the main strands of ideas and influences which have been woven into it . . .' (Ginsberg, M., *Law and Opinion in the Twentieth Century*, London, 1959, p. 320). While the substance of this study is specifically the contribution of the Labour Party to the development of English secondary education, it would be inappropriate to examine post-war developments without looking at some of these 'main strands', the social, economic and educational as well as political pressures that have operated upon Party policy-makers. It is part of our argument, of course, that the Labour Party has played a crucial role in politicizing demands for reform, but it must be admitted that it has rarely developed new ideas on its own. Certainly it required a party with certain policy predispositions to adopt the idea of comprehensive education, but, as one would expect, the original impetus came from outside the political sphere. And it is there, rather than in the Party literature, that many of the issues involved are made explicit, and it is to these we now turn.

The debate about comprehensive education, about the

problems of selection and segregation in education, has been a confused one. Its participants have included politicians, parents, administrators, teachers, educationalists, economists and educational psychologists and sociologists. It is not our concern here to evaluate in any technical sense the merits of particular arguments or theories which these groups have advanced, for most are complex, and it is doubtful whether there exists the expertise or evidence to form conclusions on them at this stage. Rather one can hope to simplify and highlight the main issues to see what light they throw on the Labour Party's contribution to the debate.

Ideological aspects of comprehensivism

English education has traditionally mirrored the English social structure. Whether or not the intention has been to stratify it on functional educational lines, the result has been stratification of the education system along the lines of social class. The association of children from different social classes with separate and qualitatively different kinds of schools, leading to different levels in the occupational and social structure, has guaranteed this. A. V. Judges has made the point that one can discern the pattern of stratification as early as 1867, when the Endowed Schools Commission was convinced by the evidence it received that English parents desired three types of education, namely: a public-school education for children destined for university and the professions; a grammar-school type of education for the children of the middle classes preparing for business; and a third level of education for children who would leave at fourteen and become artisans. As we have seen, a stratification of this sort, both between the State and private sectors and within the State sector itself, was reaffirmed by developments in the first half of the twentieth century: witness the *Hadow*, *Spens* and *Norwood Committees Reports* and the 1944 Education Act. Until the *Spens Report* in 1938 the principal division in the public sector was between the secondary and elementary schools, but that *Report* laid the foundations of stratification within the secondary sphere itself. This pattern of stratification has been a source of controversy since 1944.

The early apologists for comprehensive education in England in the immediate post-war period at first almost entirely stressed these problems of social stratification created by the education structure, and advocated the comprehensive school as a solution to them. The principal fear in the post-1944 era was that the recently reformed secondary system would perpetuate in a covert, and hence more dangerous, form the disparities in conditions and status that had existed between secondary and elementary education in the pre-war period. It was felt that different types of schools with different leaving ages would become different grades of school with superior and inferior status and, in the course of time, with different salary rates for teachers, different standards of accommodation, equipment and amenities, providing qualitatively different kinds of education preparing children for different occupational and social strata.

The reaction of the critics of tripartitism to this prospect was to press the social advantages of the common, unsegregated secondary education. While recognizing that there were clear limits to the impact that changes in education could have upon the social structure, they argued that the education system, instead of merely reflecting the society it serves, should consciously attempt to change it. This argument about the social advantages of comprehensive schools, stressing the ideological and egalitarian elements, was clearly the original motive force behind the demand for these schools, and remains so until the present time, despite the fact that it has since been complemented by more purely technical educational arguments about the inadequacies of tripartitism. The principle of the comprehensive school outlined was that, like the American high schools, they would be non-selective schools catering for all the children in the surrounding community, offering a democratic, undifferentiated education and seeking 'A common core of general education or a course of "common learning" which will unite in one cultural pattern the future carpenter, factory-worker, bishop, lawyer, sales manager, professor and garage mechanic' (Conant, *Education in a Divided World*, London, 1948, p. 87). It was thought that such an education, by drawing its members from a cross-section of the community rather than from a particular social group or ability range, and mixing freely children of different social backgrounds, interests and aspirations, would promote social unity and tolerance, encourage social mobility and lessen class-consciousness. Tripartitism, in contrast, it was stressed, although allegedly differentiating on the basis of measured intelligence, because of the established correlation of that factor with social class, was basically socially divisive.

Educational objections to tripartitism

Although it is clear that these sorts of sentiments were the original motivating force in the call for comprehensive education, they were soon complemented by more purely educational arguments. So critics of tripartitism have argued that the system is deficient in educational terms because it creates an artificial administrative barrier within what is essentially a single educational process. These arguments rest on the premise that the process of education is a natural unity that cannot effectively be broken

SELECTION AND SEGREGATION

up into arbitrary parts, depending upon a mechanical selection process to supply its different parts. Thus a one-time President of the NUT has stressed that educational needs cannot be broken into three separate categories, because they all lie essentially between two polarities. At one polarity there is 'the pursuit of language for its own intrinsic interest, the ability to relate ideas, the capacity for analysis and abstraction'. And at the other there is 'knowledge in use, relevant to present experience and applicable to a job in hand'. And if one treated education as serving the needs of society that can constitute just claims upon the individual, there would be 'no grounds for treating what is essentially one process as three or any other arbitrary number. The basic needs and claims are common to all' (King, H. R., *Inside the Comprehensive School*, London, 1958, p. 35). These needs and those lying on the continuum between them could and should, it has been argued, be catered for within one institution. Indeed, as Brian Simon has pointed out, the notion of educational diversity meaning physically separate and different institutions is a relatively recent idea, only introduced by the *Hadow Report*. And yet what it came to symbolize in the form of tripartitism was not really diversity of aims and methods, but 'a fundamental difference of educational opportunity in different types of school'.

Translated into practical terms, as Taylor has pointed out, this concern for the essential unity of the educational process led in the 1950s to a gradual loss of the natural identity of the secondary modern and technical schools, if they ever possessed one, as they attempted to imitate the standards and aims of the grammar schools. The technical schools did this by catering for more liberal studies than had originally been intended, and the secondary moderns did it by entering the same external examination system as the grammar schools, the GCE, although again it was never originally intended that they should enter external examinations of any kind. The grammar schools similarly aided the development of this process by providing more differentiation within their studies than had originally been intended and arranging more practical courses than had been foreseen in 1944. Critics of tripartitism have thus argued that, regardless of external social pressures, the system, because of its internal paradoxes, would eventually destroy itself from within. Thus only ten years after the tripartite structure had been officially legitimized, one LCC Chief Inspector noted:

> The insoluble problem of selecting pupils at the age of ten for three separate types of schools—each more or less unifunctional and each catering for a more restricted range of intelligence than it actually contains—is giving way to the problem of guiding pupils into a variety of courses given in schools, each more or less comprehensive and each overlapping to some extent the function of its neighbours (Hughes, A. G., in *Education*, 1 January, 1954).

The advocates of comprehensive education have also argued that in fact their system more fully realizes the intention of the 1944 Act to provide each child with an education consistent, not only with his ability, but also with its aptitude. In a selective system, it has been stressed, extraneous social pressures determined the content of a child's education. The demand for grammar-school education was so high that allocation of children to secondary schools was based entirely on 'ability' as measured in a formal examination, and no consideration could be given to the issue of the individual's aptitude for his allotted school, an alleged inevitability in a system where different kinds of education were given in different kinds of schools between which there was disparity of esteem. The comprehensive school, the argument runs, would avoid this problem for two reasons. In the first instance, in a system where no one kind of school had a monopoly of the best qualified staff, a large common school could provide a larger specialized staff, offering a larger range of courses and catering for a wider range of interests and aptitudes at all levels of intelligence, than could a school catering for a selection of secondary pupils. In the words of the *'Early Leaving' Report*: 'There is, or ought to be something for nearly everybody.' And in the second place, the comprehensive school could provide an education more consistent with individual aptitude because it removed the early selection process of tripartitism and substituted a general diagnostic period which would permit the progressive differentiation of studies for each individual, according to the degree and kind of ability possessed.

The evidence of sociologists

The development of an education system, however, is not dependent solely upon educational considerations. Social and economic factors also play a crucial role. Indeed, the English education system has traditionally expanded to meet the demands placed upon it by the social system it serves. And it can be argued that the combination of demands that the economic and social systems have made on the education system in post-war Britain has played one of the most important roles in boosting the notion of non-selective education at the expense of the principle of educational segregation.

The point has been made that the British education system has changed its social and economic role in the post-1944 period. Traditionally, as A. H. Halsey has argued, the education system played a 'symbolic' role in the social system, confirming rather than creating an individual's social status. But the tightening link between education and occupation in the British post-war economy has forced the education system to function more directly as 'a selector and promoter' of talent. And it has been a major criticism of the tripartite system that it has limited the capacity of the educational system to play this legitimate role. The division of education into three qualitatively different kinds of education and the association of the already privileged middle-class children with the privileged sector in the State system, i.e. the grammar schools, has tended to confine the education system to its role of confirming social status rather than allowing it to act as a generalized promoter of talent. Thus, Jean Floud has argued that the problem of the English education system is that it has been asked actually to select children for various occupational levels rather than merely giving occupational skills which can later be fitted into a fluid economy. And Taylor has made a similar criticism of the tripartite, selective system that

> the full weight of responsibility for social efficiency and individual equality is thrown on the educational and occupational selection system. There is little evidence that current selection methods, however, reliable in scholastic terms, possess sufficient long-term validity to bear this weight of responsibility (Taylor, William, *The Secondary Modern School*, London, 1961, p. 72).

Implicit in this argument is that if the education system is to be effective as a promoter of talent and an avenue of occupational and social mobility, and equally open to children of all social classes, it ought not to be primarily concerned with defining and selecting at an early age an elite which it can nurture, but rather with providing an equally valuable education for all children which would allow them all to find their appropriate place in the occupational and social structure after leaving school. This argument can obviously be justified in terms of social justice. But it may also be justified in economic terms, for, although in contemporary society education retains its significance in terms of human rights, it increases in significance as an aspect of economic development. Hence the education system cannot afford to be wholly concerned with an educational elite, as it was before 1944 and as it was in danger of becoming after 1944, since 'technological change and industrial advance do not influence an elite only; their impact is felt by all members of the society, both in their role as contributors and consumers; the work of those at every level of industry, trade and commerce is affected' (Taylor, *op. cit.*, p. 74).

These doubts about the value of educational elitism have been compounded by the sociologists' and economists' analyses of the changing nature of the industrial skills required in Britain's post-war economy. Floud, for example, has argued that the industrial demand for skills and individual abilities cannot be precisely related, because industry's demands are increasingly not for individuals who have specific skills and can fulfil only one function, but for individuals who can learn and absorb new techniques as rapidly and as efficiently as such techniques change. Thus, as Taylor has stressed, industry 'values' and rapid technological changes 'demand much greater adaptability on the part of employees, towards which a higher standard of general education can contribute a great deal' (Taylor, *op. cit.*, p. 22). Thus economic and social forces demand a more 'general' education for all pupils rather than one based on selection, segregation and specialization, the basis of the 1944 Act. That Act, it has been argued, 'was geared to a system of schools designed to serve a conception of social and industrial need that has become less and less applicable since the beginning of the fifties' (Taylor, *op. cit.*, p. 27). The conclusion has thus been drawn by Vaizey that the demand for social and industrial flexibility points the need for 'a less rigid division of secondary schools'.

Clear evidence of the growth in the acceptability of these sorts of argument is provided by the way in they pervade many official reports on education produced in the 1950s. The *Crowther Report*, for example, made the point that 'Not only in the highest grade of intelligence, where the grammar-school boy has always been able to look forward to a "career", but well down into the modern schools, it is now (or should be) apparent to all that education pays, always in the long run, and often quite quickly' (*15 to 18*, HMSO, 1959, p. 47). And yet the *Newsom Report* revealed that the talents of many children of average and below-average ability were not being utilized. This report argued that Britain's future pattern of employment would require a much larger pool of talent than was available at that time, and that much of that talent would need to come from the average and below-average pupils. 'New provision,' it stressed, 'has always elicited new responses. Intellectual talent is not a fixed quality with which we have to work, but available talent can be modified by social policy and educational approaches' (*Half Our Future*, HMSO, 1963, p. 5). Similar conclusions were reached by the *Robbins Committee*, which reflected this general belief: 'The pool of ability has always shown a readiness to expand in response to social needs several times in the past, and that it is capable of doing so once more does not seem to be in doubt' (Taylor, *op. cit.*, p. 233).

SELECTION AND SEGREGATION

Objections to selection and segregation

But possibly the greatest challenge to tripartitism has concerned the process of selection that it necessarily involves —in particular the use of intelligence tests. The advocates of comprehensive schools have always argued that if the foundation of selection, the intelligence test, is found inadequate, the whole structure of tripartitism will crumble. Their attack on the validity of selection tests has contained three basic elements. The first is whether it is possible at the age of eleven to detect individual qualities which make it educationally possible to make a valid selection for different kinds of education. The second has been the question of, even if it is possible to determine some quality upon which selection can be based, whether this is an objective quality or whether it is merely a function of social class. And the third point of attack has been, even if selection and segregation are possible in the secondary sector, whether it is not in fact detrimental to the whole of secondary education. Many of these are technically complex questions, and our aim here can only be to give a brief account of the issues involved.

LEAs use a number of techniques with which to allocate individual children to different secondary schools, but the most popular is the intelligence test, usually administered in an eleven-plus examination on one day to all children entering the secondary sector. This method of selection was developed in the 1920s, notably by Burt and Thompson, in response to LEA demands for a system of selection for secondary education more objective than those available at that time. They were intended to measure innate intelligence, which was meant to be: 'An indication of innate ability as distinguished from present scholastic performance which may reflect different degrees of educational opportunity and encouragement' (Vernon, P. E.,

Secondary School Selection, London, 1957, p. 8). However, despite a rapid growth in the post-war popularity of these techniques, there has been a corresponding growth in scepticism about their fundamental validity. The bases of this scepticism are diverse.

The structure of ability

One of the major criticisms of intelligence tests is that they are based on the assumptions of earlier psychometrists, which, as we have seen, were accepted by the pre-war committees, that one can detect at an early age in children different abilities which need to be nurtured in different institutions. They assume that intellectual, technical and practical abilities are in some sense separate and opposed to each other. But contemporary theories indicate that this is not the case. Intelligence has, among other factors, a general factor which tends to govern development and abilities, along with desirable interests and characteristics, which tend to cohere together. Intelligence tests can in fact measure this general factor at an early age. Vernon has made the point that 'the main basis of any segregation or selection must be general, all round intellectual ability, and this is what we are in fact able to measure effectively at eleven years' (Vernon, *op. cit.*, p. 39). The Swedish experience, as Husen has pointed out, has confirmed that 'practical aptitudes and also the specific group factors which, besides general ability, constitute theoretical aptitude, cannot be psychologically assessed with the same degree of certainty, and as early, as general intelligence'. But this is a quite different principle from that underlying the tripartitism of the 1944 Act, which assumed that differentiation could take place at the age of eleven on the basis of quite distinctive kinds of ability upon which a rigid allocation to different schools could

SELECTION AND SEGREGATION

take place.

A second related major criticism of intelligence tests is their implicit assumption that the intelligence they are measuring, because it is seen as an innate rather than an acquired ability, is a stable phenomenon, and that a single measurement taken at the age of eleven can form the basis of a permanent segregation of pupils. In fact, much contemporary research indicates that this is not correct. A lot of the evidence that has been collected demonstrates that abilities and performance do change over time and that children determined as both successes and failures in the eleven plus can reverse the situation in their performance at the age of fifteen in the GCE. Pedley, for example, has argued that the eleven-plus pass lists are, on the basis of his evidence, 'feeble forecasts of capacity to profit academically by a grammar-school education, the avowed aim of selection' (Pedley, R., *Comprehensive Education*, London, 1956, p. 43). And Vernon has reached similar conclusions on the stability of measured intelligence and hence the validity of selection and segregation at eleven. He states: 'it is true that correlations between intelligence test scores and measures of attainment over short periods are very high. But they sink with time, and allow of quite marked fluctuations in the abilities of a proportion of pupils' (Vernon, *op. cit.*, p. 42).

Social-class factors in educational selection

But the efficacy of intelligence testing and early selection has been criticized in the post-1944 period, not only by educational psychologists, but also by educational sociologists, who, as Asher Tropp has observed, in Britain have had a greater influence upon educational thought and educational policy than those of any other country. Their research in the 1950s raised various doubts about the

SELECTION AND SEGREGATION

effect of the 1944 Education Act on the social distribution of children attending English grammar schools. It tended to show that the proportion of working-class children attending these schools had hardly changed since before the passage of the 1944 Act, and that in fact the changes in procedure had resulted in a slight decrease in opportunity for working-class children and a corresponding increase in opportunity for those at the higher social levels. In other words, the middle classes had been the main beneficiaries of legislation which, at least in its original form conceived by the Labour Party, had been intended mainly to benefit the working classes. The 1944 Act had made a grammar-school education as available to the middle classes as it had been before the war, but it had removed the burden of having to pay fees.

Jean Floud has argued that this numerical under-representation of working-class children was not, however, a result of subjective bias on the part of administrators, but did in fact reflect the unequal distribution of measured intelligence. The problem was that the intelligence being measured was essentially not an innate but an acquired characteristic, fundamentally affected by that individual's environment, and in any test the culturally deprived child would inevitably suffer. In educational terms this still meant working-class children, for, despite the elimination of gross material inequalities in post-war Britain, the existence of fundamental differences between the social classes in life-styles, attitudes and aspirations reflected, in Floud's terms, 'a social distribution of probabilities' that working-class children would suffer in any process of early selection and segregation. The cultural privileges enjoyed by middle-class children would guarantee that they would benefit. Researchers have thus argued that the formal guarantee of equality provided by the 1944 Act was not enough, since, as the *Crowther Report* demonstrated, 'the existence of formal "equality of opportunity" does not necessarily mean that advantage will always be taken of the facilities for higher education that are available' (*15 to 18*, HMSO, 1959, p. 36).

Halsey has stressed that the concept needs to be redefined 'in a stronger sense to include the opportunity to overcome such obstacles to the development of one's ability' (Halsey, A. H., *Ability and Educational Opportunity*, OECD, 1961, p. 17). The concept of intelligence has to be seen 'less as the property of the individual and more as social or cultural products'. And this in turn meant less early differentiation and segregation on the basis of intelligence tests.

The failures of the selective system

The third argument raised against the principle of selection in secondary education is that, even if the techniques are valid, it has a detrimental effect on the education structure generally, particularly as it has been claimed that the institutions catering for the unsuccessful children who fail the selection process are inferior to those catering for the successful. As we have seen, this was an early fear expressed for the future of secondary modern schools, and one, Taylor has argued, that has been partially fulfilled. Even though more secondary moderns than grammar schools have been built since 1944, it is still possible to claim, he stresses, 'that there is a lack of parity between the treatment accorded to grammar and modern, if not in respect of basic expenditure on building at least in terms of equipment, facilities and staffing' (Taylor, *op. cit.*, p. 45). Similarly, John Vaizey has estimated that the gap between the resources spent on the two types of schools is such that the average grammar-school child receives 170% more per year than the average secondary modern child.

SELECTION AND SEGREGATION

The importance of such a situation, it has been stressed, is that it reinforces the view of parents, children and the general public that the secondary modern not only caters for the inferior, 'unsuccessful' children, but that it does so in an inferior way. This combination of fact and attitude has led the secondary modern school to be a depressing institution and, Vernon has claimed, led it to have a debilitating effect on its pupils. His research has indicated that, after three years in a secondary modern, in some cases 'children are more retarded relative to grammar-school than when they entered—not because they have learnt nothing, but because, with less pressure of examinations, homework, etc., they have not continued to learn as rapidly as have grammar-school pupils' (Vernon, *op. cit.*, pp. 43-4). And this process of stereotyping is exacerbated, he argues, when segregation is carried out between different schools rather than within a single non-selective school. Similar conclusions have been reached in Sweden, where surveys of the relative performance of children in selective schools, schools for those who have failed the selection process and wholly non-selective schools have revealed, in the words of one commentator, that 'There seems to be no pedagogical advantage in grouping pupils of average and below average ability, since the developing of skills in children of comparable intelligence in such classes is less favourable than in undifferentiated classes' (Husen, in *Ability and Educational Opportunity*, *op. cit.*, p. 132).

Critics of segregation have thus argued that it is socially and educationally unjust to pass off less intelligent children into schools which are inferior to selective schools. The issue is, of course, essentially one about social justice, and raises the question of for what ends and for whose benefit secondary education should be organized. If secondary education is seen principally as a training ground for university entrants, it can be organized to fulfil this exclusive function. If, however, the needs of the vast majority of pupils who do not enter sixth forms and universities are to be considered equally important, a different emphasis would need to be placed on organization. For a highly selective system is never without costs for the less intelligent.

We have seen that the roots of the movement against selection and segregation in education are complex. They are important because they form the intellectual environment within which Labour Party policy-makers have operated. They are ideological as well as purely educational, and consist in part of historical reaction as well as theoretical conviction. The advocates of comprehensive education have thus been able to use a variety of these arguments to support their case. It is clear, however, that the original dynamic force in the demand for these schools was a concern for social justice and the problem of the socially and educationally deprived child, rather than the technical educational disadvantages of tripartitism, although, of course, many of these have confirmed the social injustices inherent in tripartitism. The educational arguments are no doubt valid, and pedagogues and parents can be concerned about individual injustices. Political parties, however, need greater motivation than this, and it is obvious that the Labour Party, whatever it may have claimed, has primarily been interested in comprehensive education for its impact on the social-class structure. The Party was originally attracted to it from its concern to maximize the educational opportunities of the working classes, and this has remained its primary source of interest in the issue. Despite employing other justifications for its policies, the Party has adopted the principle of comprehensive education for its ideological and egalitarian implications.

5
The Labour Party and the comprehensive school, 1951-65

Reappraisal of the Labour administration

The Party left office with its attitudes to comprehensive education unclear. Official Party policy, on the other hand, appeared a little more certain. As we have seen, the last years of Labour office had been critical for the Minister of Education as both the mass movement and then the NEC itself moved to oppose Ministerial policy of only limited experiment with comprehensive schools. The shift in opinion was finally marked by the publication in 1951 of *Secondary Education for All*. That document committed the Party to a policy of comprehensive reorganization. There was little evidence of any internal opposition to this stand. Indeed, there was little attention paid to the issue in the immediate period after Labour left office. It had not at that time become a feature of Party conflict, and education generally fell into the backwaters of daily politics.

The open commitment to the comprehensive school remained Party policy, however, and received its confirmation at the 1952 Conference from the NEC spokesman, Alice Bacon. At the same time, however, she clearly expressed the NEC fear that the chances of getting comprehensive reorganization were diminishing as the passage of time sanctioned the developing tripartite system, and she urged Labour-controlled LEAs in particular to take more note of Conference decisions in this respect and hasten the development of a comprehensive system. She rightly made the point that the passage of the 1944 Act had made many Labour LEAs reluctant to disturb the tripartite system, for it had appeared to have had the approval of the National Party. And at the same time it had made the Party itself a little complacent, too willing to rest content with the admittedly major advances that had been made. The NEC, however, was anxious not to remain immobile in education, and set up a Social Services Subcommittee to review the whole educational structure on the grounds that there remained 'a great deal of fundamental reconstruction' to be done before equality of opportunity could be realized.

The new proposals and their critics

That Sub-committee reported in March 1953. It confirmed Alice Bacon's earlier arguments that Labour's plans in the post-war period had not been very challenging precisely because 'it seemed to be assumed that the application of the 1944 Act would be sufficient task for the Labour Government'. Yet it argued that, because that system was essentially elitist in nature, educating a minority to lead and the majority to serve, it was incumbent on the Party to change it. 'Not only does Socialist principle demand it,' it was stressed, but 'electorally a policy which showed how to do away with the gross inequality of the present school system could win a great deal of popularity.'

The precise details of their plans for comprehensive development were, however, to create some difficulties within the Party. The NEC appeared to reject as impractical the orthodox all-age comprehensive school that had been principally developed by the Labour-controlled LCC, and instead opted for a split system of junior and senior comprehensive schools. The latter would cater for those children who stayed on beyond the statutory leaving age. It was intended to contain classes, not only for pupils going on to university, but also for technical and commercial students. Nevertheless, the impression was created that the NEC wanted the best of both worlds, i.e. common unsegregated education to fifteen and yet the preservation of an educational elite beyond that age, a policy which seemed destined for trouble, in view of previous Party commitments. The conclusions of the Sub-committee were substantially accepted by the NEC, and were published in a policy document, *Learning to Live*.

The plan came under heavy fire before it even reached the Annual Conference. The debate at the Annual Conference of the NALT most clearly indicated the precise nature of some members' fears about the plans. The powerful arguments they raised against the scheme were that they would lessen the number of working-class children staying on at school beyond the statutory leaving age, since parental, social and economic pressures would prevent many from making the transfer to senior school at fifteen; that this would in turn reduce the opportunities of working-class children to compete for higher-paid jobs by virtually putting the GCE out of their reach; that it would further divide the teaching profession; that it would increase rather than decrease social distinctions, since the gap between the ordinary school-leaver and senior school-leaver would be even greater than that existing between the grammar schools and secondary modern schools; and, finally, that it would delay the raising of the school age to sixteen by creating a natural administrative break at fifteen.

Similarly, there was a great deal of criticism of the plan at this stage in the columns of the *New Statesman*. Michael Stewart probably made the most telling point here when he argued that in fact it was essentially a question of bad tactics by the NEC, and that a majority of Party members would have accepted the proposals if they had been made in association with an overt, positive commitment to the principle of comprehensive education and had merely been suggested as one possible solution to the practical and administrative problems involved in reorganization, rather than as the Party's optimum solution.

And when the Conference came to consider the document it reached essentially the same conclusions. Despite the rear-guard action of a minority of members who feared that the comprehensive schools would decrease the educational opportunities of working-class children, it decided that the NEC proposals were foreign to the principle of comprehensive schools, which essentially involved a common, unsegregated education for all children of school age. And after the attack had been pressed home by a large number of delegates the NEC agreed to redraft the offending section on the basis of an NALT amendment calling for the all-age, orthodox comprehensive school. The new version was published later in the year, when it was revealed that the NEC had taken Stewart's advice. The split system was retained in a minor position as one sort of solution, but a clear commitment was made to the principle of the all-age school. As the TES noted at the time, the Party once more appeared united on priorities. And this, of course, was important. For even if the prospects of returning to power and implementing a national comprehensive policy were clearly not good, the Party was able to affect the development of the secondary system through Labour-controlled LEAs, which gave the debate an immediate, practical significance as well as a long-term theoretical importance. In fact, this issue had another significance, in the sense that it was to become a problem once more when the Party eventually came to office in 1964, as will be seen later.

The Conservatives' view of comprehensives

While this internal controversy was being resolved, there was a general lack of Party conflict on the issue. The Party was confined to token Parliamentary opposition to the Conservative Government's policy, whose commitment to tripartitism at this time was almost total. The Minister's general attitude was that there were no educational advantages attached to the comprehensive schools which could possibly outweigh their disadvantages in terms of size 'to the children, to the teachers and the whole organization'. The Ministry was prepared to sanction limited experiment with comprehensive schools if the LEAs first suggested the proposals, but it would not initiate reorganization. If comprehensive experiments did take place, they had to be set in the context of a set of selective schools, and so arranged that they could be dismantled and reorganized as separate schools if that should later prove desirable. At all costs, parental choice of school had to be maintained.

But, as Labour argued, comprehensives could never succeed as merely one element in a basically selective system, where, in fact, parental choice had long been superseded by a formal examination structure. And their worst fears were confirmed when in 1953 the Minister refused to sanction the merger of an LCC grammar school with an existing comprehensive school, solely on the grounds that it would change the nature and status of the grammar school. Employing these criteria, the Party could see that all LEA developments in the direction of comprehensives could be permanently blocked by the Ministry.

The Minister's successor continued to espouse the same

general principles. His view was that at that time the grammar-school stream in the nation's schools could not be enlarged beyond the prevailing limits without radically altering the whole character of the university and grammar-school system, a development which could not be tolerated. The solution to parental demand for grammar-school places he argued, was an improvement in the conditions and status of the secondary modern schools. While unable to justify the retention of the eleven-plus system as it stood, he refused to accept a solution which would mean the death of 1,200 good grammar schools and reveal to parents and teachers a lack of confidence in the secondary moderns. But essentially the Ministry rested its case on the need for variety of provision and a degree of choice for both parents and LEAs. Its general criticism of Labour's policy was that it was attempting to impose a uniform, central pattern on LEAs at a time when only twenty-three out of 146 of them had proposed the development of comprehensives and only six had plans for total comprehensivization.

In fact, it was probably an effective policy for the Conservatives to attack Labour for advocating comprehensives on ideological grounds at this time. For, despite the many educational arguments that could be made in favour of comprehensive reorganization, Labour spokesmen at this time generally tended to emphasize the social virtues of the schools at the expense of educational considerations. This no doubt reflected Labour's real interest in the issue, and could possibly be applauded in ideological terms, but it did tend to make its policy vulnerable to attack on the grounds that it was politically motivated.

Problems of presenting the policy to the electorate

There is evidence to show, however, that at this time the

Party was beginning to pay more attention to these sorts of problems. The two problems it was most concerned about was how to present their policies to the electorate while in opposition and then how to implement the policies when it came to office. On both these issues they were divided. Margaret Cole opened the debate in an ACE memo. in January 1953. In this she argued that the Party's first priority ought to be to get itself internally united on the issue before attempting to convert a sceptical public, especially since 'the lukewarmness of the two Labour Ministers of Education, together with the unwillingness of some Labour-controlled LEAs to carry out Labour's own policy, has made a universal programme impossible, since it is no part of Labour's intention to force LEAs to embark on new experiments'. This conclusion that compulsion ought not to be used was endorsed by Joan Simon, who argued that, instead, the Party should rely upon a huge publicity campaign to convert the public, with local Labour groups and the Labour Minister pressing for comprehensive reorganization.

The NALT, however, did not share this point of view, and argued that if Labour wished to implement its plans at some stage it would have to introduce legislation. A similar line was pursued a little later by the Publicity and Policy Sub-committee, which stressed that the Party's most recent policy statement had been silent on three crucial problems which the Party would have to resolve. These were whether a Labour Government would abolish the eleven-plus examination within the first five years of its office or leave until later in its ten-year programme, whether the comprehensive principle would be put into practice immediately or whether LEAs would be given five or ten years to reorganize, and, finally, what sanctions if any, such as the withdrawing of grants, a Labour Minister would be prepared to employ on LEAs that refused to conform. The Sub-committee's own conclusion was that at some stage a Labour Government would have to be prepared to make comprehensive schools compulsory within a given period.

A similarly hard line was being pressed by Alice Bacon, who argued in 1955 that the Party could afford to be more dogmatic on the issue, because the general public and Party members were more interested in the idea of comprehensive schools than they had previously been, and that in the case of the Party the only disagreement was about 'the speed at which we should proceed and the means by which we should put our policy into operation'. And while she recognized that some members were doubtful about interfering with the autonomy of LEAs, she stressed the point that if a Labour Government allowed LEAs to do entirely as they wished it would have no national policy, a point appreciated by Conservative Ministers, who had always been prepared to prevent the local establishment of comprehensive schools.

In the event, however, the Party lost the 1955 election, and the critical test of its intention was deferred to a later date. After this defeat, at the next Conference the NEC submitted a proposal to spend the following three years developing policy documents in detail over a range of areas, including education. Next year the Sub-committee produced an interim general statement of policy, *Towards Equality*, the most traditionally radical document of the decade. Without developing any policies specifically for education, this made a blistering attack on the inegalitarian consequences of tripartitism. But once again it demonstrated that the Party had not as yet appreciated the electoral benefits of stressing the educational or economic advantages of non-selective education, as opposed to its advantages in terms of social or class justice.

At this time the Conservative Minister of Education

LABOUR PARTY AND COMPREHENSIVE SCHOOL

produced an interesting response to the Labour Party's critique of tripartitism and the secondary modern element in particular. His argument was that Labour's allegations about the inferiority of the secondary moderns were disproved by the fact that the traditional indicators of the middle-class status of grammar schools, that they led to an income beyond the necessities of life, that they were the only schools leading to salaried posts, and that they alone had intellectual interests, were in fact being eroded. The Minister suggested that economic developments in the 1950s had reduced the gap between salaries and wages to such an extent that in the first place one could not differentiate the parents of children in grammar schools from those in secondary moderns, which would reduce the disparity of esteem attached to the different kinds of school. The second result was that pupils of both schools were competing for equally well-paid jobs, which again reduced the social distinctions alleged to exist between the schools. For both these reasons, it was not necessary to carry out more than minor adjustments to the tripartite system.

It is interesting to compare this analysis of contemporary socio-economic developments with one made at the same time by a future Labour Minister of Education, Anthony Crosland. The differences between them clearly highlight the differences between the two parties' attitudes to the role of education in this period. While agreeing with the Minister's analysis of economic changes that had taken place in the 1950s, Crosland reached entirely different conclusions about their significance for the education system. His argument was that it was precisely because these changes had taken place and that social rather than crude economic factors now created and sustained social-class divisions, that the education system had become crucial in post-war Britain. As economic indices of social class had become less important, the differences in social status conferred by the education system had become more so. This in turn meant that, far from ignoring the differences that were created by the tripartite structure, the Government should attempt to eliminate them by developing comprehensive education.

At this time the future Minister was advocating a fairly soft line on reorganization. Given that a Labour Government would not be starting *tabula rasa*, and that it would not wish to coerce the vast majority of LEAs who had not reorganized, his policy would not entail the ending of well-established grammar schools. There would be three main points of attack in his programme, but all were very conciliatory in tone. The Government would make a positive commitment to comprehensives and do more to encourage LEAs to experiment with them. It would reduce the disparity of esteem between schools by channelling more resources into secondary moderns and breaking the unique grammar-school link with superior occupations by extending the GCE to secondary moderns. Finally, a Labour government would further reduce disparity of esteem by raising the statutory leaving age to sixteen, making the *de jure* leaving age at secondary moderns the same as the *de facto* level in grammar schools. It is interesting to note that when Crosland eventually came to office, events had moved so far as to make these conciliatory proposals quite outdated.

Strategies for implementing the policies

The debate on the presentation and implementation of a comprehensive policy continued in 1957. In May Michael Stewart submitted a memo. arguing that the Party still needed to do much more explanation and propagandizing of the policy, both within the Party and within the electorate, if a Labour Government was to have sufficient support to be able to implement it. To do that it should start immediately a general policy of collecting and recording information from LEAs and Labour groups on councils on how to implement their plans locally, since 'even though a wholesale and rapid transformation was not possible, every effort should be made to get the process effectively started'.

The relevance of these proposals was demonstrated by the results of a public opinion poll carried out for the Party in that year on the public's attitude to reform in the State and private sectors of education. The survey revealed two important facts for the Party. In the first place, it showed that the vast majority of the public were ignorant of the issues involved in comprehensive education. And, second, it showed that only 10% of the sample, anyway, felt that segregated education was socially undesirable, although working-class parents felt more strongly about this than did those from the middle classes. The majority of parents were basically satisfied with the existing education system, and, while there was a strong desire for traditional changes, such as the reduction of the size of classes, there was practically none for radical reorganization.

In the first case, the group decided that the absence of public knowledge of and apparent interest in the issue of comprehensive education meant that continuous propaganda, sustained well beyond the next election, would be necessary if the Party was to establish a public demand for, or at least acceptance of, their policy. But the results of the survey also affected the kind of propaganda they felt the Party should pursue. The group argued that the real appeal of the comprehensives probably lay in stressing, not the egalitarian virtues of the schools, but rather the opportunities they offered to all children who could benefit from it of getting a grammar-school education and a variety of opportunities for the rest. Its general conclusion was that 'a policy argued around conventional educational opportunities is bound to have considerable popularity. One which argues on manifestly doctrinal or egalitarian grounds would prove unpopular even among our own supporters.'

The year 1957 appeared to be one of general uncertainty for those involved in making policy in education. A further memo. in June of that year would tend to confirm this. This recognized the degree of local opposition to comprehensive education, and argued that the Party would need to weigh very carefully how and whether it would use compulsion to enforce LEAs to reorganize, 'often against very strong and sincere opposition from Labour local authorities', as well as to decide what sanctions would or should be used on recalcitrant religious authorities. At the same time, the memo. raised the practical difficulties involved in the orthodox all-age school and resurrected the notion of split junior/senior comprehensive schools that had been so decisively rejected four years earlier. In fact, a number of Party members, notably Alice Bacon, were arguing that public and Party were more likely to accept this plan at this stage as the difficulties in reorganization became more apparent. This was to some extent confirmed by resolutions sent to the Conference in 1957, which, although not debated, noting the difficulties attached to the orthodox all-age school, indicated that alternative quasi-comprehensive plans of the Pedley variety would be 'equally satisfactory'.

At the end of the year the study group on education set up in 1955 was beginning to reach its conclusions. It attempted to deal with a number of ambiguities in Party policy in two main areas. It first made the point that previous Party statements had not been anxious to pose its comprehensive policy in terms of the disappearance of the grammar schools, and that the Party would have to decide whether it could retain this confusion in future statements. If it did not consider it possible to do this, it would need to estimate what would be the impact of a clear statement on the possible ending of the grammar schools, both upon Party members and upon the public at large. At the same time the memo. dealt with the question of sanctions for LEAs, but was unable to resolve the issue. It was decided not to enforce compulsory patterns, but to allow LEAs to develop a variety of plans to meet local needs, which could be submitted for approval. But this in itself was ambiguous and did not indicate the extent of variety the Party would tolerate.

A further memo. submitted a little later in the year spelt out the relative advantages and disadvantages of this issue a little more explicitly. The objections to legislation which would enforce reorganization, it argued, were that the Party would be accused of interfering with the autonomy of LEAs, that it might affect the special agreement with voluntary schools, and that it would lead to long and violent controversy in Parliament. However, the advantages of legislation would be that the Party could ensure that the basis of comprehensive education was laid in its first period of office, and that it would then be more difficult for a future Conservative Government to reverse that decision.

The results of these internal deliberations were revealed in *Learning to Live*, published in 1958. That attention had been paid to the results of the Abrams survey was shown by the fact that its main attack in the State sector was not on tripartitism, but rested on the less overtly ideological argument that the major defect of the secondary system was the result of insufficient resources being devoted to it.

However, while not given a very prominent place, the proposals for comprehensives were nevertheless very interesting. The essential point was that, although the advantages of the normal all-age school were admitted, it was stressed that this was not the only arrangement at the secondary stage whereby children could be provided with 'the real opportunity for real choice'. The important point to ensure, it was argued, was not that there was one particular form of school, but that the comprehensive principle was guaranteed. Many local authorities had experimented with different forms of non-selective education, and Party policy would not be to exclude these developments, but 'to examine the extent to which the developments favoured by several authorities of bilateral, multilateral and campus schools begin to approach the comprehensive principle'.

Retreat from rigour

In fact, a noticeable softening of Party policy had been taking place during the months before publication of the pamphlet. A report in the TES at this time indicated that not all the Party Leaders felt that the orthodox school was the answer to the problem. And Gaitskell confirmed this in a public speech, where he gave a much wider definition to the term 'comprehensive' than any of his colleagues previously had, arguing that it did not mean that all children should attend the same kind of huge, impersonal school, 'but something much simpler than that, that we abandon the idea of permanent segregation'. As the TES report observed, this meant that, put in these terms, the policy of a future Labour Government would be uncertain. The burden of the Party's argument seemed to be now against the finality of selection at eleven, and beyond that many arrangements would be permissible. Strangely enough, however, not a dissident voice was heard on these proposals at the 1958 Conference, which was admittedly preoccupied with the public schools. Whether this silence was born of uncertainty or of a new realism in the Party or a combination of both of these is not clear.

Support for the former view came in a book published at the time by Roy Jenkins, *The Labour Case*. In this he admitted that the existence of a network of grammar schools over the country had led to 'some difference of opinion' in the Party as to what their future relationship with a comprehensive system should be. His own view, and it was one that he suggested was shared by a number of Party members, was that, given the Party would not be starting *tabula rasa* and could not implement a system 'almost entirely on a comprehensive basis', good, established grammar schools should be preserved as a bridge between the State sector and the private sector. The comprehensive schools would play a limited role in his scheme, since they would only be created where new schools were to be built or reorganization was necessary for other reasons. This restricted role for comprehensives was also envisaged by Emmanuel Shinwell, who once remarked:

> We are afraid to tackle the public schools to which wealthy people send their sons, but at the same time we are ready to throw overboard the grammar schools, which are for many working-class boys the stepping-stones to universities and a useful career. I would rather abandon Eton, Winchester, Harrow and all the rest of them than sacrifice the advantage of the grammar school.

It is apparent at this time, then, that views differed on the proper role of comprehensive schools, varying from the limited role advocated by Jenkins to demands for legislation for rapid, universal, compulsory comprehensivization. In fact, *Learning to Live*, published in 1958, came out at least against a public explicit declaration of a policy of legislation. It also seemed to give up the idea that reorganization could be wholly achieved within the first five years of office, and admitted that it would in fact take many years for this to be achieved. A Labour Government would, however, require LEAs to prepare development plans 'with all reasonable speed' to adopt the comprehensive principle. The fact that legislation was not to be imposed, however, did not mean that a Labour Government would allow wholesale opposition to its declared policy, for, as the NEC spokesman, James Griffith, remarked of Labour's attitude to recalcitrant LEAs, 'it is for the nation, through Parliament, to decide what should be the national system of education. Local authorities cannot be allowed to contract out of it.'

The Party was similarly ambivalent on the question of the future of the grammar schools. The 1958 policy statement tried to reconcile two points of view by arguing that, although the comprehensive principle would mean the demise of the grammar school as a separate institution, the important elements of it would be retained in a different form. They offered, in Gaitskell's phrase, 'grammar-school education for all'. But although the Party was to persist in this policy, it is unlikely that it concealed the essential fact from the general public that existing grammar schools would be changed in nature and status, which was essentially the basis of local opposition to reorganization. It is difficult to disagree with Boyle's remark on this point that a grammar school was 'a selective school which caters for a definite range of ability', and for the Party to argue otherwise was at least disingenuous.

There can be no doubt, however, that continuous Labour pressure, both at national and local level throughout the 1950s, was instrumental in shifting the Conservative Government a little closer to acceptance of at least some of the principles of unsegregated education. Indeed, in response to Gaitskell's speech on comprehensive education in 1959, the Minister, Lloyd, suggested that, since Labour was merely defining comprehensive education as a system wherein children were not finally segregated at the age of eleven, 'the comprehensive principle in this form is warmly acceptable to us'. But essentially as the White Paper, *Secondary Education for All*, published in this year revealed, the Conservative Party assumed a very limited role for comprehensives. Even if they were successful, the Paper stressed, 'it would be unwise to regard them as anything but exceptional'. Experiments could take place in limited areas, but the idea of plans which would end existing grammar schools simply to give comprehensive schools a monopoly of an area were quite unacceptable. The Conservative Government was not even prepared to accept Labour's suggestion to set up a research committee to examine the possibilities of such schools.

National deadlock

After 1959 the issue of comprehensive schools seemed to become less prominent as a political issue. In a sense, this was to be expected. The parties had long since formulated their general policies, and little that either could say or do was likely to produce a marked alteration in the policy of the other. Any attempted reconciliation was bound to falter on the rock of selection and segregation. No matter how close the two might appear to come, the fact that Labour could not admit that this process should continue, and the refusal of the Conservative Party to abandon it, meant that the gap between the two was essentially unbridgeable. Even the apparent shift from rigour on this question by Labour in 1959 could not conceal this fundamental disagreement. Nationally, the two parties were at stalemate. The real debate over comprehensive education was shifted from the national to a local level as the issue began to be worked out in practical terms. As Greenwood remarked at the 1960 Conference, the NEC was planning a tremendous campaign to put across the idea of comprehensive education, and it was looking 'to the Labour groups to be the spearhead of the attack which we hope will be waged'.

Although the comprehensive issue seemed to become less prominent nationally at this time, there was an interesting shift in this period in the sort of propaganda the Party began to use for the schools. Previously, as we have seen, the Party tended to put the issue very much in ideological or class terms, stressing the socially inegalitarian nature of the tripartite system. However, as the 1957 survey had shown, the presentation of the issue in those terms was not likely to prove electorally attractive. Initially, this had led the Party to play down the whole issue, but at this time in the early 1960s the realization appeared to dawn that they could continue to publicize their policy if they posed it less in terms of the social justice and more in terms of the direct economic advantages that could be gained from a system of unsegregated education. This style of presentation was very much favoured by the new leader, Harold Wilson, who, in his now famous 'Science and Socialism' speech to the 1963 Conference, laid great stress on the point that the Party opposed a segregated, elitist secondary system, not only because it was unjust and socially divisive, but also because, by failing to capture talent at the point of entry to secondary education, it held back Britain's technological development and operated against our success in economic affairs. There can be no doubt that this line of approach was to prove electorally popular. Nor can there be any doubt that some of these ideas are to some extent valid. To what extent they reflect

Labour's real interest in comprehensive education is, however, open to question.

The Labour Government

The election of a Labour Government in 1964 reopened all the old controversies about comprehensive education. For our purposes, there were three significant interrelated issues: the timing of reorganization, the pattern of reorganization and the use of compulsion. As was seen earlier, the question of the future role of grammar schools had been a problem for the Party ever since the 1945 Labour Government, both for its electoral implications and also because of the emotional attachment to them demonstrated by some Party members.

The first issue the Government faced was the question of the timing of reorganization. We have seen that the Party had always been anxious to go a long way in laying the foundations of a comprehensive policy during the first five years of its office, and public policy was that the LEAs should be asked to submit reorganization plans within a specified period. Both Ministers adhered to this policy of a fairly rapid reorganization. Crosland, however, to some extent revealed a degree of uncertainty about the implications of this policy. For example, on being appointed Minister in January 1965, he observed that, because the road ahead was 'studded with obstacles, the shortage of public buildings, the state of public opinion, and the fact of local self-determination', comprehensive reorganization would be introduced at a moderate pace. There would be no question of a sudden closing of grammar schools nor the rapid conversion of secondary moderns into comprehensive schools. The intention of the Government was to encourage LEAs to be 'more audacious' in experimenting with comprehensives. Yet three weeks later he was reported as saying: 'I believe, however, that in five years' time such progress could be made that the comprehensive system would be accepted as the normal pattern, towards which all local authorities were working, though necessarily at different speeds.' In a way, the Government was in an impossible dilemma over this point. It realized that it might only be in office for five years, and had to speed up the process of reorganization. But at the same time, given the nature of the relationship of the Ministry with the LEAs and the real practical difficulties, it could not force the pace too quickly.

The Government, however, seemed to find the solution to both this question and the issue of compulsion in the same set of events. More or less immediately on taking office, it claimed that to a large extent the initiative for reform had been taken from it by the passage of events, as LEAs had been independently developing comprehensive schools, and that its policy was merely to regain some control of affairs. Crosland, for example, stressed that the movement against the eleven plus towards comprehensive schools 'had not been politically inspired or imposed from the centre', but had rather been 'a spontaneous growth at the grass roots of education'. It was 'precisely because this movement of reform was gathering such strength in the country that it was necessary to develop some form of central guidance and supervision . . .'. It was because of the fact, Stewart had argued, that during this spontaneous movement there was the danger 'that we may get a number of ill-tried experiments and the further problem that we cannot afford too great a degree of local variation in the country, as otherwise it is very inconvenient for parents who move about, that I believe it is now right for the central Government to give a clear lead on this question'. There had to be 'some limit to the time which we can wait, the time which we can consult'. Thus the question of withdrawing of grants or the possible use of legislation was not resolved at this time. In a sense, the Ministry decided to see how far it could manage reorganization by using its traditional tactics of persuasion. The advantage of hindsight and the variable response from local authorities would confirm the opinions of some members in the 1950s that compulsory legislation would at some point be necessary as the process of trying to implement change by Ministry circular proved inadequate. But probably the Labour Government felt that to try to work by consensus, the traditional approach in education policy, was the best approach at this stage. Probably it felt it would at least lay the foundations of comprehensive reorganization in this way in a majority of LEAs, in which case it could afford to delay the issue in the case of a minority of unwilling LEAs.

In July 1965 the Ministry issued Circular 10/65, which *inter alia* laid down the intended pattern of LEA comprehensive reorganization. In keeping with the previous debate, the policy was presented as a kind of inevitability, with the central Government obliged to enter the arena to rationalize an ongoing process. In keeping with previous policy—and one could make the point that policy was deficient in this respect—the circular recognized as acceptable a variety of forms of comprehensive organization. In all, six were admitted. They were: (1) the orthodox all-age school; (2) a two-tier system of junior and senior schools with entry to the senior school at the age of fourteen; (3) a similar two-tier system where not all the pupils were transferred at fourteen, but some remained in the junior school and left at fifteen without taking public examinations; (4) a two-tier system where at thirteen or fourteen the pupils went to one of two senior schools, depending on whether they intended to attend beyond the statutory leaving age; (5) a common school from eleven to sixteen combined with a sixth-form college for pupils over sixteen; and, finally, (6) a system of middle schools straddling the primary-secondary age-ranges, dealing with pupils from nine to thirteen, before sending them to a comprehensive senior school. Despite the fact that all these plans were recognized, the Minister did not uniformly favour them all. Solutions (3) and (4) were to be temporary expedients only. It could be argued that the Party, while in Opposition, did not devote enough attention to this problem of the pattern of reorganization. Again, however, it was in a difficult situation. On the one hand, the dangers that by allowing LEAs so much freedom in choosing a pattern of reorganization they could defeat the intention of comprehensive principle of common, unsegregated secondary education was self-evident. Permitting LEAs to develop sixth-form colleges would be a good example of this danger. One recalls the debate in 1953 on precisely this issue. And, of course, this danger was exaggerated by the need for a rapid reorganization, which meant that many LEA plans could be submitted to and approved by the DES as fulfilling their general criteria when this might not be the case. But again, given the Party's situation, that it might only be five years in office, and the fact that the physical conditions and arrangements of schools varied so much between LEAs, it is difficult to see what else could have been done. Once again the argument would probably be that if the process of reorganization was started early, despite the individual anomalies, it would be so entrenched administratively and politically that it would be extremely difficult for a Conservative Government to reverse the process.

The publication of this circular marks the end of the period under review. It also marks the end of two decades of internal Party debate about the structure of English secondary education. This was a period which was markedly more controversial than the pre-war period, when the task of the Party lay in converting the educational establishment to the idea of universal secondary education. There internal disagreement over Party policy was rare and rapidly resolved. The post-war period has been quite different. As we saw, the Party itself was for some time uncertain about the policies it should adopt and precisely how it should implement them. And no doubt pockets of resistance still remain. Thus on the one hand its task has been to convert internal critics and to reconcile a variety of opinions on the presentation of policy. At the same time it is clear that the other aspect of its task, that of moulding public and professional opinion in favour of its policies, has been much more controversial than was the case before 1944. The world of education itself has been uncertain of the issues involved, and the different protagonists cannot be clearly divided into radicals and reactionaries, as was to some extent possible in the case of the programme for universal secondary education. But in general it can be argued that the Labour Party has handled both these problems quite successfully. Clearly, it has done enough to unify internal opinion and carry its policy. The problem of converting public opinion has been more difficult, but, given the inherent controversial nature of the principle of comprehensive education and the complexity of the administrative aspects of reorganization, the Party has had reasonable success.

6
Labour and private education

A system of private education is not peculiar to Britain, but it is the country where the system has traditionally been most influential. The existence of such a sector provides us with a good opportunity to examine the concerns and priorities of the Labour Party's education programme. Private education, and the public schools in particular, have constituted a classic affront to the moral, social and political values of the Party. The existence of such an area of alleged educational and social privilege has long led both Party members and supporters to demand that the Party 'do' something positive and radical to limit its significance. But at the same time such demands for action have raised a series of political, moral, educational and administrative dilemmas for the Party, which has resulted in moral anguish for many members, and more important in ambiguities in Party policy. The purpose of this chapter is to throw some light on the problems faced by the party in this area and some of the solutions they have formulated.

Early Party opposition

In fact, the issue of private education has received a lot of attention from writers not normally interested in the process of educational reform. But a great deal of this literature has been directed towards solving some of the internal problems of the private-education structure, rather than the problem of changing the more important feature of the system's relationship with the broader social structure. The advocates of change were generally proponents who were concerned to conserve private education. In this sense, Mack was right in his argument that 'the modern movement to reform the public schools becomes essentially a struggle between the ideas of Labour, summed up in the word "liberalism", and those of upper-class defenders of the public school' (Mack, E. C., *The Public Schools and Public Opinion*, London, 1941, Vol. 2, p. 326). In the nineteenth century the private sector needed protection from its friends; it was not until the mid-twentieth century that it found itself in need of protection from its enemies.

The Labour Party has clearly traditionally been an enemy of the private sector of education, but its capacity and willingness to express its hostility in a practical form have differed in different periods. In one sense one can find evidence of Labour opposition to the public schools from the earliest days, but it can also be argued that such opposition has essentially, and probably necessarily, been symbolic in nature. It can be argued that, despite its theoretical opposition to private education, the Party never saw itself in any position to change the situation until the 1940s, by which time the system was being forced to change itself.

Early Conference reports make explicit the Party's opposition to private education. For example, the 1907 Conference committed itself to pressing for 'A national system of education under full popular control, free and secular from the primary school to the university'. And Conferences in 1913 and 1922 pressed for enquiries into all educational endowments, expressing the common

Labour belief that the original endowments for public schools had been usurped by being made available to the children of the middle classes, since they had originally been intended for the education of poor scholars. The essence of this argument was that 'money had been taken from the poor people and was now being used to educate the aristocracy in order to make them fit to govern the poor'.

The failure to act

But it cannot be suggested that these expressions of sentiment in any sense added up to a coherent policy for the private sector. In fact, the period 1918-40 was remarkable for the absence of practical policy proposals from the Party, in view of its declared opposition to the private schools. During this time there was not one policy pamphlet, nor one memo. from the ACE, nor more than one major Parliamentary debate that gave any indication that the Party had developed any coherent policies for private education. On only one occasion did the issue assume any practical political significance, and even on that occasion it was limited.

The Labour Government of 1923-4 took no measures at all which related to the private sector. The issue was never the subject of Ministerial statement, let alone action, nor was action ever urged by any member of the party at large. The second Labour Government did, however, take some steps to deal with one minor aspect of the problem. A number of Labour MPs were anxious to remedy various administrative defects in the system governing the operation of private schools, and brought pressure upon Trevelyan to legislate on the compulsory registration and inspection of these schools. After a period of reluctance when he argued there were many other more important matters for a Labour Minister to be dealing with, he eventually acquiesced in the setting up in 1930 of a Departmental Inquiry on the registration and inspection of private schools under Chuter Ede, one of the Labour Members who had originally pressed the case. But it was clear from the start that the intention of the Inquiry was to remedy an administrative anomaly and to rationalize the private sector of education rather than to challenge the existing structure. It in no sense constituted an attack on the entrenched position of private schools.

The Committee did, however, reach the conclusions expected of it by Labour MPs. It revealed that of the estimated 10,000 private schools catering for 400,000 pupils, none was subject to compulsory inspection, and in practice only a few were inspected on a voluntary basis. Many schools were found to be excellent, but a small proportion were so defective that they were harmful to the mental and physical welfare of their pupils. In a mildly reformist vein, the Committee argued that the Board's powers of inspection and powers to close unsatisfactory schools should be increased. But when it reported in 1932 the Party was no longer in office and, despite the protests of Labour MPs, successive Conservative Presidents argued that legislation on the topic would be too contentious and too time-consuming and ignored the *Report*.

It cannot be argued, however, that the failure of the Board to act on the proposals much affected the position of the private sector. The *Report* never claimed more than to be dealing with the periphery of the problem of educational privilege. It did not deal with the essence of the problem which was the social intake of private schools, their relationship with the State sector of education, their relations with the universities or their broader links with the occupational and social structure. And in no sense could it be considered a basis upon which the Party could develop a coherent policy for private education.

An explanation of this absence of a coherent Party policy for private education, and indeed the absence of any evidence of consistent Party concern for the problems of the private sector, was attempted by Tawney in an important memo. submitted to the ACE in 1941. Arguing that in fact a plan for private education 'ought before this time to have been included in the educational programme of the Party', he attributed the absence of policy proposals to two main factors. The first and most important was that while Labour educational reformers had long been aware of and concerned about the problem of private education, they had been too concerned with pressing for reforms in the State sector, which, after all, was concerned with the children of the Party's constituents, the working classes, to have had much interest to spare for schools commonly believed to exist for the exclusive benefit of a small, wealthy class. The second reason was that the fact that many public schools were not aided by the State, together with the powerful social influence exercised by their leading representatives, had prevented them from becoming the target of public controversy. The result was that the private system had generally been regarded by Labour people as a closed world, interference with which would encounter tenacious opposition. And the problem had never been given priority for Party action.

The issue reopened

In fact, the question of reform of the public schools which began in earnest in the late 1930s was not raised in the political sector at all, but by the schools themselves. A series of factors combined to confront the public schools with difficulties, which, if not new, were raised for them

LABOUR AND PRIVATE EDUCATION

in a more acute form than ever before. In the first place, the fall in the birth-rate began to affect them as well as all other schools. Second, the considerable improvement in State education, in both quality and quantity, had led parents to question the educational superiority of the schools. And, finally, the crisis of the war reduced family resources and led parents to doubt the worth of an expensive education, especially since the status of private education in the post-war situation was growing increasingly uncertain. The result was that many of the schools, because of a drop in demand, were forced to reappraise their once-impregnable situation.

The solution they reached was to apply to the Board to see what financial aid it was prepared to offer in return for a number of places in their schools being made available for State pupils. This policy produced an immediate reaction from the Party. The first debate for many years on private education took place in March 1940, where it was confirmed that the revival of Party interest had been caused by the crisis that the schools were undergoing, one that for the first time raised the possibility of their dependence on State funds. In the debate the ex-President Lees revealed that it was the intention of the Party to take this opportunity to reform the schools. As he aptly remarked:

> So long as public schools can stand on their own feet, so long will they be unassailable, but if they propose to put themselves upon the taxes they must be prepared to meet the claim that they should revert to their original purpose of being schools for their people, for which most of their foundations were initially provided.

There could, in Labour's view, be no public aid without public control and public entry. The public schools would have to accept a large proportion of children from public

99

elementary schools, a figure which would have to increase until it reached a very substantial number in a limited period of time.

Thus the prospect of public financial aid for private education raised the problem for the Party for the first time in an acute practical form. Tawney had already recognized this possibility in his memo. to the ACE. The prospect of financial aid, he felt, raised two related questions for the Party. The first was whether it should acquiesce in the idea of payment at all, and the second was what conditions should it insist upon if payment was made. He personally rejected the view held by some members that the issue should be ignored as being either too difficult or too trivial, and argued the case for immediate action, especially since it was unlikely that a time would occur again when the general public, parents and the schools themselves would all simultaneously recognize the need for action.

The general proposals for change being made at this time, especially by the schools themselves through the heads of public schools, basically assumed the continuation of the schools playing a similar educational and social role under slightly changed conditions. They principally involved making the schools available to boys of small means, assisting the schools from public funds and creating closer links between the schools, the LEAs and the central government. Tawney argued that if the Party were to agree to a scheme along these lines it should insist upon five points: that the solution be made by all parties involved and not foisted on the LEAs by the schools and the central government; that not all schools should be automatically given a grant, but that research should first be undergone into the extent of the need for boarding education; that the schools should be equally available to all children from elementary schools and not clever working-class children; that LEAs should support day-boys, but that the central Government should support boarders; and, finally, that there should be close co-operation between the schools and the LEAs so that the schools could be obliged to comply with State secondary regulations. The latter he regarded as an important step in bridging the gap between the State and private sectors, ensuring more representative governing bodies, LEA control and inspection of school endowments, and Board control of the numbers of day-boys and special places and also of entrance examinations.

These changes were intended to improve the situation in three ways. It would ensure that half the pupils in boarding schools were day-boys, and would thus help to break the boarding-school mystique. It would bring the schools within the State system. And it would end the schools as a privilege of an elite class. This scheme did, however, have two real disadvantages for the Party. In the first place, it was voluntary, and as such not bound to encompass the best and most financially successful schools. And in the second place it assumed the continuation of the schools in a basically unchanged condition. It did not question their educational or social role in any fundamental sense. Nevertheless, Tawney felt that if the proposals did not go very far to satisfy egalitarian requirements, they represented a wedge that could later be driven into the system of privilege.

These proposals have been considered in some detail, not because they immediately became a guide to Party action, but because they represent the first serious Labour proposals developed during this period. They provide an insight into the mind of Labour's most prominent educationalist at a time when important decisions were being taken that could vitally affect the future shape of English secondary education. The interesting point is, of course, that the proposals were so moderate; in no sense were they as radical as his earlier programme on the State sector.

The Fleming Report and Party reaction

The Party as a whole was soon to get an opportunity to express itself on the issues involved. The general uncertainty surrounding the future of the public schools in the late 1930s had led the President of the Board to appoint in July 1942 the Fleming Committee 'To consider means whereby the association between the public schools . . . and the general educational system of the country could be developed and extended'. The Committee produced its report in 1944. Once more fundamental questions about the role of the public schools were not really asked. The Committee produced a well-meaning *Report* attempting to associate the State and public schools, based on the assumption that recruitment from the State to the public schools would bridge the gap between the two systems and resolve the problem of privilege.

In essence, the scheme was that the public schools participating would offer 25% of their total places to pupils who had spent at least two years in State-aided primary schools. The Board and the LEAs would grant bursaries to qualified pupils to cover the remission of tuition and boarding fees and other expenses. The scheme of admission was to be reviewed every five years with a view to 'the progressive application of the principle that schools should be equally accessible to all pupils and that no child otherwise qualified shall be excluded solely owing to lack of means'. And to this end the progressive increase from 25% of State bursaries was planned.

There were, however, two main flaws in the proposals which vitiated their prospect of implementation. In the first case it did not adequately deal with the problem of the criteria to be employed in the selection of State bursars. It was stressed that the criteria were not to be wholly intellectual, but nor were bursars to be sent to a school where the standard of work was beyond their capacities or the curriculum not suited to their needs. The Regional Boards making the choice were to be guided by the parents' choice of school and by 'the special needs and aptitudes of the pupil'. These were sufficiently vague so as never to make clear which group of children the Committee thought should legitimately attend public schools. But more important, as it turned out, was that the scheme was wholly voluntary for both the schools and the LEAs. There was thus no sanction for not participating in the scheme and, one suspects, not enough incentive offered to encourage it.

Strangely, in view of the pressure that had built up for reform before the *Report*, it received a muted reception. In fact, the Party revealed very little interest in the Committee's proposals. This was confirmed at a later date in 1948 by an NEC spokesman, Harold Clay, a member of the Fleming Committee, who in reply to a number of Conference critics of the public schools argued that it was a pity that the Party 'was not a little more active in connection with fee-paying when the majority *Report* of the Fleming Committee was published, because that was a time when we might have gone substantially further than we have done with regard to the remission of fees if we had had the support from the Movement that those of us who had signed the majority report thought we were entitled to'.

A number of factors can help to explain the absence of Party interest in the Fleming proposals. In the first case it can be suggested that the Party indulged its usual habit of concentrating on reforms of the State system at the expense of the private sector. The 1944 Act absorbed much of the enthusiasm for educational reform and probably diverted a lot of attention away from the public-school issue. On the other hand, it can be argued that those groups of people on the left of the Party who might have been expected to force the pace of reform had in fact lost interest in the proposals even before they were published, because it was clear that they would necessarily be moderate, piecemeal, administrative adjustments. Thus Cove of the NALT, in advance of publication, had rejected any solution which he felt would bolster the public schools, deprive the State schools of their brightest people and 'make working-class children into snobs'. And so the reaction of the Party to the Fleming proposals was almost entirely negative.

The Labour Government

And when Labour came to office in 1945 reform of the public schools did not feature in its programme at all. Essentially, the problem was that the Fleming scheme had left the initiative for reform in the hands of the LEAs, who were reluctant to pay bursaries when it meant that a minority of children would receive an expensive education at the expense of the majority of the LEA pupils. As a result, there was no lead from the LEAs, nor any from the Labour left, nor any from the Labour Government, which was preoccupied with reform in the State sector.

In fact, the only mildly controversial aspect of Labour policy in this field was concerned with the future of the direct-grant schools. At the time of the *Fleming Report* and the Education Act, Labour Members had pressed for the abolition of all fees in all State schools, but eventually they had reluctantly acquiesced in the 1944 arrangement, where a number of schools of direct-grant status were provided for, on the assumption that it was the only one Parliament would accept. When a Labour Minister was returned to office MPs pressed once more to abolish the schools, or at least to wait until LEAs had made clear how much secondary accommodation they could offer before sanctioning the retention of any direct-grant schools. Ellen Wilkinson's attitude to the issue was ambiguous. While admitting that Labour MPs had only reluctantly accepted the arrangement in 1944, she decided to retain it, although operated under rather more stringent conditions. In the first place, in keeping with her views on the State sector, she wished to retain variety and flexibility in education. But apart from this she argued that, despite the Party's wish to make education as free as possible, the fact that 50% of the places were free as far as parents were concerned and that the other 50% were open to competition meant that entry had in fact been democratized. Nevertheless, she wished to make the criteria of direct-grant status quite rigorous, and argued that in the absence of any special educational features, she saw no reason why many existing direct-grant schools should not become free secondary schools under the LEAs. The net result of her policy was that whereas in 1938 there had been 237 direct-grant schools, in 1948 this had been reduced to 165. But this, of course, did not satisfy her critics on either side. More radical Party members criticized her for being too moderate, while the Conservatives accused her of breaking faith with the agreement contracted by the Caretaker Government. But at least a small blow at educational privilege had been struck.

But advocates of public-school reform received even less encouragement from her successor, George Tomlinson. Indeed, on one occasion, when pressed by his critics, he admitted that he thought the Fleming proposals impractical as a guide to action and on another, through his PPS, explained that where boarding education could not be provided by the LEAs, they should have the freedom to use the private sector for that purpose. Although it was later explained that the use of these plans was not meant as an alternative, but rather as a 'valuable addition' to LEA boarding schools, the impression nevertheless remained with some Party members that the Minister had publicly condoned State patronage of private education. Whether this was true or not, the Minister throughout his reign remained complacent on the issues involved in private education.

The Party itself was, however, at this time less certain of the policy it should pursue for private education. A memo. to the ACE early in 1947 explored the policy alternatives open to them. It pointed out that the existence of a private education system, recruiting its pupils on social and financial rather than educational grounds, possessing many advantages in building standards, staffing ratios and closed scholarships to the universities, was anathema to many socialists, who were pressing for reform. But on the other hand it recognized that many Party members felt it was not 'compatible with the British idea of liberty to refuse to allow educational institutions outside the State system to exist'. The compromise solution of Fleming, however, it was felt, carried with it the dangers of bolstering the private system at the expense of the State secondary system and the public taxpayer. Its own recommendation was that the Party should concentrate on raising the standards in the genuinely public schools, so that eventually only 'snobs and fools' would continue to patronize the public schools, at which point the problem would be resolved. And this was the policy adopted by the Party in the policy pamphlet published for that year.

This temporizing attitude was even more clearly revealed by the Minister in a memo. he wrote in 1948 on the development of education in the years 1950-5. In this he argued that 'nationalization' of the schools at that time 'would not be worth the very considerable opposition it would arouse', especially since their significance as a stronghold of privilege was 'steadily diminishing', as representation by the Ministry on the governing bodies and the admission of an increasing number of State pupils approved and assisted by the LEAs was bringing the schools within reach of deserving pupils irrespective of income. His final point was that 'from the point of view of the floating voter I am quite sure that any other solution [apart from infiltration] would carry with it disadvantages quite outweighing any benefits'.

And as the Ministry progressed, less and less attention came to be paid to the issue of the public schools. As we have seen, the principal actors whom one would have expected to press for developments were not interested in the contemporary solutions for a variety of reasons. The process was, of course, aided by the fact that during the years 1948-51 the internal debate on the future of comprehensive education was coming to a climax, and this necessarily absorbed most of the interest of the reformers. And after a decade which had promised so much, in which a Labour Government had been in power for five years, the position of private education generally and the public schools in particular remained as untouched and as intractable in 1951 as ever it had been in the eyes of the Party.

Return to Opposition and reappraisal

The return to Opposition in 1951 led the Party in education, as in many other fields, to a general reappraisal of its policies. The first-fruits of this process were contained in their new policy statement published in 1953, *Challenge to Britain*. But the policy presented represented no change on the Labour administration's policies. It remained as cautious as ever. The manifesto made clear that, although the relative conditions of the State and private schools make a mockery of the notion of equality of opportunity in education, the Labour attack would concentrate in the first instance not on abolishing the fee-paying schools, but on improving the standards of free education. In the private sector the Party would confine itself to intensifying the inspection system and introducing a licensing system.

The policy statement was welcomed by the TES for its spirits of liberalism, but understandably received a very different reception from the Annual Conference that year. The general reaction of the majority of speakers was unconcealed hostility to a programme that placed a solution to the public-school issue outside the next ten years' work. The amendment calling for the Party to adopt a policy wholly compatible with socialist belief which meant that 'all fee-paying in schools will be abolished and all public and private schools will be taken over by the nation immediately Labour returns to office' received a wide measure of support.

An interesting contribution was made to the debate by the future leader of the Party, Hugh Gaitskell. While agreeing with the critics of the NEC about the absence of any intention to act on the matter, he argued that the Party should avoid getting itself the image of an authoritarian Party which consistently closed things down. His proposal was that the public schools should be treated like universities, the prerogative of intellectually gifted children. That this was in many senses a contradiction of the Party's policy for comprehensive secondary education and that the plan would anger some members of the NEC did not concern him too much, his point being that 'if we are going to keep them, if we are going to have some kind of education, it should be segregated based on brains and not wealth'.

This meritocratic argument, which reflected the discussion there had been in the State sector about the future of grammar schools under comprehensive reorganization, was a difficult one for the Party. And it was one that the NEC spokesman, Alice Bacon, was at pains to refute on this occasion. The NEC, it was made clear, could not accept total abolition of all private education, since this would unfairly discriminate against preparatory and experimental schools which were essentially peripheral to the problem of the social divisiveness of the public schools. But nor could it accept Gaitskell's proposals, which would be a financial burden on the LEAs, as well as involving them in invidious selection procedures. Essentially, the NEC's point was that the greatest sense of public grievance was caused by the inequalities within the State sector, which contained 95% of the nation's children, rather than by the inequalities between the State and private sectors when the latter contained only 5% of the school population. And it was eventually their arguments which prevailed at the vote, despite the earlier criticism there had been of their policies.

It was clear, however, that this endorsement of NEC policy was not going to resolve the issue. The internal dialogue was to continue in private and public in the period to follow. The dilemma was a real one for the Party, and it gave rise to a variety of responses. Michael Stewart, for example, was at this time arguing that, despite the recent Conference decision, the next Labour government should spend only five years developing the State sector and mobilizing opinion in favour of abolishing public schools, and that at the end of that time the government should simply acquire them and use them for its own diverse purposes. A memo. to the Policy and Publicity Sub-committee in 1955 argued on this point that *Challenge to Britain* had left this position unclear, and that the NEC would have to clarify it before the next election, despite its own admission that 'there will be no agreement on this subject by education experts within the Party'. In the event, however, no attempt was made to clarify the issue—indeed, the Party's electoral programme made no mention of it, confirming Alice Bacon's assessment of the situation that 'We just don't know what to do with them'.

The conflict intensifies

Towards Equality, however, published in 1956, appeared to show that the Party was becoming a little more certain. In contrast to its predecessors, this document argued that the divisions between the State and private sectors of education were at least as significant as those that existed within the State sector itself, since their broad effect was 'to heighten social barriers, to stimulate class-consciousness and to foster social snobbery'. Its conclusion was that a classless society and the existing pattern of education could not be reconciled, and that action was needed on the public schools. Well received by the Conference of that year, this radical policy seemed to stimulate critics on the left even more in the following months. The process was started by a memo. from Margaret Cole and Michael Stewart which argued that, although the Party could ignore the private sector and concentrate on the State sector, this could have no real effect on the problem within twenty years, and that if the Party did decide to pursue such a policy 'we must recognize frankly that we do so because of the difficulty of doing anything else and that we are leaving across the road to equality a huge obstacle which will not melt away of its own accord, but must sooner or later be moved'.

A further memo. a month later was designed to summarize and crystallize the Party's general position on private education. This first defined the basis of the Party's traditional opposition to the public schools. This was that they exercised an inordinate amount of social influence; that they created a two-tier system which made the State system appear inferior; that they had considerable educational advantages; that their curriculum was too academic and unsuited to the needs of British society; that they created employment and recruitment problems; and, finally, that their advantages could be bought rather than acquired on the basis of merit. On the other hand, it also clarified the Party's traditional reasons for not dealing with the issue. These were that the public schools affected a small minority of children; that it was easier to close the gap between the two systems by improving the public sector; and that they were essentially a middle-class educational problem, and that tampering with them could only raise a great deal of opposition without benefiting any large proportion of the child population. But primarily this research paper was concerned with the ethical problem of whether it was permissible in a democratic State to prevent parents from buying services beyond those provided by the State. Pointing out that all the legislation of the 1945-51 Labour Government had left alternatives to the State services intact, it concluded that 'the whole problem is essentially one that agitates the middle classes . . . to abolish private education altogether would be physically and administratively difficult and it is doubtful whether it can be ethically justified in a democratic society'.

And it was this ethical problem that was later taken up by Richard Crossman. In a memo. he also made the point that it was doubtful whether it was in fact democratic or desirable for the State to have a total monopoly of education, but that this alone did not preclude the Party taking action of some sort against the private sector. The solution was not the Fleming plan, because its advocates had never solved the related problems of the criteria of selection, the probable middle-class dominance of the free-place system or the size of LEA expenditure required for each State bursar.

His own solution involved a variety of proposals concerned primarily with breaking the patterns of privilege associated with private education. One would be a more rigorous application of Part 3 of the 1944 Act to root out bad private schools. A second would be to abolish the category of direct grant schools, thus ending fee-paying in State schools. In addition, LEAs should have their powers to purchase places at private schools curtailed. But the suggestion he considered most important was to break the nexus between the public schools and Oxbridge, for, he argued, it was the selection network for Oxford and Cambridge colleges that gave the public schools one of their most important privileges. Accordingly, he proposed to abolish fee-paying in all universities, to insist that entry to Oxbridge colleges should be by university examination, over which the individual colleges would have no control, and to develop a plan whereby it might be possible to ration the number of day and boarding schools so that they only received their fair share of places in relation to the State sector. In this way it was hoped, if not to eliminate public schools, at least to eliminate their real social and political signifiance.

In the last months of 1957 opinions wavered as the conflict between the preservationists and abolitionists grew more intense. The report of the Party's opinion poll appeared to strengthen the case for inaction. This showed that the majority of parents were not anxious for change on ideological grounds, either in the State or private sector of education. Only 8% of the respondents wanted to abolish the public schools and 50% wanted to leave them wholly unaltered. Indeed, 52% of them wanted their own children to attend a public school, 80% of all parents were prepared to pay for educational privilege, and less than 20% opposed such expenditure on ideological grounds. This latter figure was only 23% among Labour supporters.

Thus, on the grounds of electoral expediency, as well as on those of ethical and administrative difficulties, a policy of *laissez faire* recommended itself to the Party. Its dilemma was commented upon in a memo. by Tawney, who, noting the opposition that action on the public schools would arouse and the effect of such opposition on Labour's plans for the State sector, commented: 'It is a problem whether a Labour government would be justified in jeopardizing the remainder of that programme for the sake of only a part of it, however important in itself, concerned with the future of the independent schools.'

The advocates of reform were not, however, deterred by such considerations. In December memos. were submitted by Stewart, Peart and Mulley, all demanding action by the Party. They demanded at least a progressive democratization, starting with 75% of places being made free at selected schools, and in the strongest form asked for a commission that would negotiate with LEAs with a view to taking over completely selected independent schools, day and boarding. All these plans assumed the end of the category of direct-grant schools, but a Conference of Labour educationalists held in February 1958 demonstrated the dangers of that sort of policy.

LABOUR AND PRIVATE EDUCATION

The general view of the Conference, which was addressed by, among others, Hugh Gaitskell, was that to withdraw the direct grant would be disastrous politically and educationally. The real difficulty was that, given that it supported the comprehensive school, the Party could not at the same time defend the selective direct-grant schools. Yet at the same time it could hardly attack the more 'democratic' side of private education and leave untouched the public schools, as it apparently wanted to. Their general conclusion was that on balance 'under the present circumstances the public schools were best left alone, in which case it would be folly to launch an attack against the direct-grant schools'.

When *Learning to Live* was published in 1958 it was shown that the forces pressing for inaction had prevailed. A long and detailed statement stressed the difficulties involved in taking any action on the public schools. The main reasons for not acting were that abolition could be no guarantee that new institutions would not arise to take the place of the prohibited schools, and that it would also constitute an unjustifiable encroachment on individual liberty. The arguments against democratization were the problems of selection, the costs involved for the State and the dangers of bolstering up middle-class institutions at the expense of the public taxpayer. Similarly, no action was to be taken on the direct-grant schools, although the list would not be allowed to increase, and at some future stage it might even be reduced.

Conference reaction to this policy was extremely hostile, particularly in view of the promises that had been made in the 1956 policy statement. An amendment, moved by Peart, substantially argued that LEAs ought to take over all direct-grant schools in their area, that fee-paying should be abolished in all schools and that all independent schools should be integrated into the State system and made available as part of a general educational plan. It received strong support from the delegates. The NEC spokesman, Alice Bacon, in her reply, however, argued, not in terms of the social morality of the situation, but in terms of the practical problems involved in the Party taking any action. The private sector was easy to attack, she pointed out, but what the Party needed was 'a sound, workable and acceptable policy'. And eventually the amendment was defeated, the Conference drawing back from a decision which would bind a future Labour government to passing legislation making it 'illegal for any parents to spend any money whatsoever on the private education of their children'.

The need for action accepted

Nevertheless, it was clear to the NEC after this that any policy which was to be acceptable to majority opinion, as revealed at successive Conferences, would have to promise action of some sort on the public schools. After the Conference the NEC set up a sub-committee to reconsider the problem. Reporting the following year, this reaffirmed the Party's opposition to private education in principle, but remained as divided as ever on a practical solution. It eventually sent forward a variety of proposals for the NEC to consider, its own preference being for a policy of gradualism. The NEC was dissatisfied with the ambivalence of the report, and committed it to a group of leading members for consideration. Their proposals were eventually produced in *Signposts for the Sixties*, published in 1961.

In contrast to the previous policy statement and in keeping with Conference demands, the Party now claimed that it was convinced that 'the nation should now take the decision to end the social inequalities and educational anomalies arising from the existence of a highly individual and privileged private sector of education outside the State system'. It proposed the creation of an Educational Trust, which, after full consultation with the local authorities and the schools themselves on method and timing, would 'recommend the form of integration that will enable each of them to make its best educational contribution'. The integrated schools could fulfil a variety of purposes. Some could become sixth-form colleges. Others could serve the needs of areas which could not provide schools with a sufficiently varied range of courses. Others could remain as secondary boarding schools for children whose parents' cirumstances made that type of education necessary. A few might be used to meet the demands of the eighteen-twenty-one age-group for an education less advanced than university level. Thus, while promising action, the plan was essentially a moderate one designed to integrate rather than abolish the public schools. Clearly, if the NEC was going to promise action, it was not going to the length demanded by some critics.

The Labour Government and the Public Schools Commission

This was the last major shift in Party policy before the Party came to office in 1964. From this point on the Party publicly and consistently advocated positive action in the private sector. Of course, the question now became what priority it would attach to reform when in office, for this was clearly an area of policy where it could postpone action more easily than it could in the State sector. The appointment of Crosland as successor to Stewart as Minister gave at least some indicator of the Party's purpose in this issue. He was a well-known advocate of reform of the public schools, as both his books, *The Future of*

Socialism and *The Conservative Enemy*, testify, and his appointment meant that at least pressure would be brought to bear for reform. And in office the Minister confirmed the promise of his earlier writings. In March 1965, for example, he threatened action against the schools, and compulsion if necessary. While rejecting both the thesis that the problem should be ignored and the other that all schools should be abolished, he promised: 'I want to go as far as I can by agreement, though not, of course, ruling out legislation altogether. . . . It must in the last resort be the Government's responsibility to ensure that pecuniary privilege gives way to equal opportunity over the whole field of education.'

After some delay in appointing the Chairman, the Public Schools Commission was set up in December 1965. On announcing its creation to Parliament, Crosland explained that 'The Government are determined that the public schools should make the maximum contribution to meeting the educational need of the country, and that this should be done in a way as to reduce the socially divisive effect which they now exert'.

As the terms of reference of the Commission subsequently confirmed, he implied that any solution would have to ensure that the schools would become progressively open to children, irrespective of their parents' wealth; that a wider range of educational achievement should be accommodated so they could play their part in the shift towards comprehensive education; and that any unsatisfied needs for boarding education amongst wider sections of the population would be met. The Commission would be expected to collect information on the need and existing provision for boarding-school education, to work out roles that public schools could play in national and local schemes for integration, and to recommend a national plan for integrating schools with the maintained sector of education.

But, despite the information it has produced, it is difficult to avoid the conclusion that this arrangement was essentially decided upon because the Party could not resolve its own internal difficulties. Whether the intention was to delay action or acquire Establishment blessing for possibly unpopular policies, it is difficult to see what this sort of Commission could add to the Party's existing store of information on the issue of private education. As we have seen, the Party has been conducting enquiries into the general problems for over twenty-five years, and the problem has never been one of a shortage of proposals, but of a failure to choose between unpalatable alternatives. And it is unlikely that this solution will make the decision any easier to take when the appropriate time comes.

But this particular action is in many ways symptomatic of the Party's behaviour throughout this period. It has always wanted to act on the issue of private education for a variety of reasons, but the problems attached to any course of action have always seemed too great. And in this sense Tawney probably best summarized the position of the Party when he questioned whether the Party could afford to risk sacrificing the vast bulk of its programme of educational reform for the sake of a minor, if controversial, piece. Generally, the Party has not drawn back from potentially unpopular or controversial policies in the State sector. The fact that it tended to do so in this issue probably tells us more of its educational priorities than it does about the limits of its radicalism.

7
Conclusion

This study has been essentially an historical narrative of the Labour Party's contribution to the development of English secondary education. It has examined some of the problems faced by the Party in this area and the solutions it has developed. In many ways, a formal conclusion, as opposed to a general summary, is superfluous. At the same time, however, there are a number of general points one could make at this stage.

Perhaps one should start by attempting to draw the individual chapters together in a general assessment of the impact the Party has had on secondary education.

Of course, it is dangerous to account for changes in the education system solely in terms of the activities of a single political party. The process is clearly more complex than this, and is a function of the interplay of a number of social, political and economic forces. But this does not mean that one cannot attempt to evaluate the relative contribution the Labour Party has made. And at least in this way one can question the assumptions of educational historians who have emphasized too often the purely administrative aspects of educational developments and have neglected the crucial role political factors have played in the process of change.

But at the same time it is difficult to know what criteria to employ in judging the Party's record. If one were to

CONCLUSION

assess it solely in relation to the claims it has made, or the educational goals it has prescribed, or even more in relation to the demands of some left-wing members of the Party, one might conclude that on some issues it has fallen short in its achievement. The difficulties over the introduction of the comprehensive school in 1945-51 or the failure to press the reform of the public schools would be two clear examples of this. If, however, one steps out of the immediate Party context and assesses its contribution to the development of secondary education in relation to those made by other political or social groups, then a different picture would emerge, and its contribution would seem to be much greater. It is again dangerous to pose the question: What would the English secondary system look like now if the Labour Party had never existed? The answer is that we do not know, and it is quite possible that similar changes would have taken place in a different context. Nevertheless, to ask the question does oblige us to look at the contribution of the Labour Party in the most positive way. For example, although the record of the Conservative Party has not been examined in great detail, it is clear that if its philosophy alone had governed the development of English education the pattern would be quite different from that which exists today. In view of its ideas about the nature and role of the secondary education system in the pre-1944 period, it is likely that the implementation of universal secondary education would have been delayed beyond 1944. Similarly, its views on the desirability of selective education would also have probably meant that a universal system of comprehensive education would not have been implemented, but that some combination of selective and non-selective schools would have been developed. And whatever the results of the present deliberations on reform of the public schools, it is clear that the Conservative

CONCLUSION

Party would not have initiated any such reform in this sector.

When seen in this context, it is clear from our study that the Labour Party has made an important contribution to the development of English secondary education, despite the fact that there has often been internal disagreement about the direction of Party policy. At the least, the Party has been an ally of the forces of progress and reform. We saw that in the pre-1944 period the Party adopted and consistently pursued a radical policy of universal secondary education, which was eventually to form the basis of the 1944 Education Act, arguably the most important piece of educational legislation this century. In the post-war period the Party played an exclusive political role in propagandizing the concept of non-selective education, and so helped to change the climate of public, and to a degree professional, opinion that the Labour Government was eventually able to order the reorganization of English secondary education. And in the sphere of private education, although a number of specific criticisms could be made of Party policy, it has nevertheless played a role in publicizing the issue of educational and social privilege, which in itself has been valuable.

The point that has emerged from this study, in fact, is that the Party has played a peculiar pressure-group role in educational policy-making. While it has generally not been in a position to enforce decisions in education, it has nevertheless exercised a considerable effect on the direction of development. Especially in the issues of secondary education for all and comprehensive education, it has politicized demands for reform so effectively that practically all its policies have been implemented. Clearly, in neither case was it the only social force exerting pressure for change, and one cannot ignore the role

CONCLUSION

of such factors as the activities of professional organizations, the changing views of Conservative politicians, changing economic and social needs, developments in educational theory or adverse international comparisons. But still the contribution of the Party in terms of both creating demands for change in education, while at the same time focusing existing demands for change in the policy-making arena, remains a large one. The fact, as Glass has observed, that policy-making in education is a cumulative process, where change rarely occurs until a consensus is reached, has, of course, provided the Labour Party with the situation and opportunity to play an influential role in policy-formation. And, of course, the fact that the machinery of education policy-making is a partnership, which has allowed Labour-controlled LEAs to affect developments in education even while the national Party has been in opposition, has also helped.

In the Introduction to this study, it was suggested that parties should be best regarded as policy-making bodies which do have general policy predispositions which motivate their behaviour. It should be clear from this study at least that the Labour Party does operate in this way. Throughout the fairly lengthy period we have examined there has been a remarkable general consistency in Party concerns in education. In the first case, Labour Party policy in Opposition has always consisted of more than electoral slogans. It has, in fact, attempted to act as an alternative governing party by developing in Opposition policies that were meant to be implemented once in office. And in office it has generally attempted to follow those policies. Both the pre-war minority governments, the Attlee Government and the present administration have attempted to give practical expression to the demands they formed in Opposition. Of course, the most obvious exception to this was the controversy in the 1945-51

CONCLUSION

period over the introduction of comprehensive schools. But in this case, as we saw, a reasonable explanation could be made for this policy. Basically, the controversy could be related back to the Party's pre-war achievements and the passage of the 1944 Education Act. Its very success in getting accepted the principle of universal secondary education prevented the Party from realizing that the traditional notion of what constituted equality of opportunity in education, upon which the 1944 act was based, was being criticized as inadequate, even as that Act was still being implemented. Eventually, of course, the assumptions upon which the Act was based were to be supplanted by a stronger definition of equality, which was to include a far greater awareness of the importance of social factors on educational selection. On balance, however, it can be argued that, in view of the importance of this issue and its crucial impact on English education, the Labour Party was remarkably quick to assimilate the new ideas and incorporate them into its own policies.

There has been a further source of consistency of Party concern in education in the sense that its programme has always been intended to increase equality of opportunity in education. The desire to change the existing arrangements for more egalitarian ones, and hence improve the opportunities of working-class children, must be seen as the motive force of the Party's policies for secondary education for all, comprehensive reorganization and public-school reform. Its arguments have not merely emphasized the individual inequalities and injustices of the English secondary structure, but more importantly the social-class inequalities. This concern for social as opposed to individual justice is quite overt in its policy of secondary education for all and the issue of public-school reform. These policies have been designed to improve the educational opportunities of working-class

CONCLUSION

children. And although it has been less overt in the case of comprehensive reorganization, and the Party often claimed that it was more concerned about the individual justice than the middle-class monopoly of the grammar schools, there can be no doubt that its adoption of that policy was motivated by concern for the interests of working-class children. This was particularly clear, for example, in the immediate post-war period, when Party opinion only seriously mobilized around the possibilities of comprehensive education as the realization grew that, contrary to its expectations, secondary education for all in the form of tripartitism actually penalized working-class children.

Moreover, the Party has pressed these egalitarian policies even when they have not necessarily been electorally popular. For example, demands to extend secondary education in the 1920s and 1930s were not popular with many of the working class, who felt unable to make the economic sacrifices involved. Nor was its decision to abandon the grammar schools wholly acceptable to many of its working-class supporters with middle-class educational aspirations. And attacks on the private sector have only served to alienate the majority of the middle classes without necessarily attracting the support of the working classes, who were generally more concerned with the inequalities within the State sector. In fact, the question of the impact of electoral considerations upon Party policies is an interesting one. Obviously, having accepted the need to operate within a Parliamentary system, the Party has been socialized into accepting the need of anticipating the electoral consequences of particularly policy decisions. But it is the point at which such anticipation begins substantially to affect policies which is most interesting.

Clearly, it can be seen that, at least in this policy area,

CONCLUSION

considerations of electoral advantage have never been the most important factor in policy decisions. But it does appear to be the case that electoral considerations became more prominent the more complex any particular decision was. For example, the question of whether to pursue a comprehensive policy in the period 1945-51 was internally controversial for a variety of reasons. But when advocates on both sides were unable to convince their opponents on educational grounds, they resorted to stressing the likely electoral consequences of their opponent's policies. However, when the internal differences were resolved in the early 1950s, little attention was paid to these electoral consequences, even though they were known to be controversial in some degree at least. And even when in 1957 the public opinion poll pointed out some of the dangers of its policies, it had very little real impact on subsequent policy. Similarly, the issue of public-school reform raised a number of problems for the Party which it was unable to solve. And, again, one found that when unable to convince their opponents with other arguments, the protagonists began to emphasize the electoral implications of particular policy decisions. Hence these considerations were given more prominence than they merited, although in fact they were probably more objectively potent in this issue than was the case with comprehensive reorganization. For although the Party appeared prepared to sacrifice some electoral advantage if it could lay the foundations of a universal comprehensive system, it was far less willing to risk losing support and the opportunity to pursue reform in the State sector to reform the public schools.

There are, however, perhaps two general criticisms that should be made of the Party's record in education. The first may be considered an ideological one, but it is not directly intended to be so. It concerns the question of

CONCLUSION

reform of the public schools. Much of the chapter on this subject was devoted to an explanation of the Party's failure to take positive action in this field. And it is to be hoped that the account made clear the reasons for this failure to act. Explanation, however, was not intended to imply approval. For, despite the complexity of the issues involved, it can be asked whether the Party, given its general predispositions, ought not to have risked the consequences (which it possibly exaggerated) and to have pursued a radical policy in this area. It is probably fair to say that the Party, by concentrating on the quantitative aspects of the problem, has underestimated the need for an attack on the problems of social and educational privilege exhibited by those schools. Arguably, the issue was as much a challenge to its idealism as was tripartitism, and the need for consistency alone would probably demand some radical action. On the whole, its record in this field of private education has less justification than its record in the State sector.

The second criticism may be considered a little unfair in the sense that it could probably be applied to either party, rather than specifically to the Labour Party. But the point still needs to be made. It is that the Party has not shown a sufficient understanding of the sociological aspects of educational change, and has thought too much in terms of legislative and administrative changes. As we have seen, in the post-1944 period the Party assumed that changing the institutional framework would guarantee a reform of the education system, and this in a sense proved to be unfounded. Similarly, it could be argued that the Party has tended to assume that by ending the institutions of tripartitism it has guaranteed the success of comprehensive education. But this is clearly not true. Many other social and economic factors will determine the success or failure of this movement, and the issue is by no means

CONCLUSION

resolved merely by administrative changes. One can argue in this sense that the Party has oversimplified the problems in creating educational changes. And the emphasis the Party has laid on the quantitative aspects of the public-school problem, in an effort to minimize the significance of the issue, while to some extent neglecting the important qualitative social issues, would probably confirm this judgment.

At the same time, however, it must be recognized that any party in government has only limited tools to effect immediate social changes. If, for example, it wants to create changes in the social role of the education system, in the short term it can do little other than change the institutional framework. It can hope to encourage the desired developments within a changed framework, but it cannot directly create changes in the social, political and economic value structure of a community which would guarantee the success of institutional reforms. In this sense the Labour Party would inevitably be a little simplistic in its attitude to educational change. But if the Party has been more guilty than the Conservative Party of underestimating the problem involved in change, this is because in the final analysis Labour has been more concerned about educational reform.

Finally, one can say that a relatively coherent picture has emerged from this study of the contribution the Labour Party has made to the development of at least one important aspect of English education. Despite inevitable internal disagreements, the Party has been consistent both in its long-term goals and in its demands for change, both in office and in Opposition. It has persistently exercised pressure for reforms intended to make English secondary education less elitist and class-oriented. And, despite the relative infrequency of its periods in office, it has been an effective advocate for reform. Whatever criticism may

CONCLUSION

be made of Party policy from members of the left or opponents on the right, and there are many, its contribution to English education remains a major one.

Suggestions for further reading

This section is intended to draw the attention of the student to those books already included in the bibliography which would serve as an introduction to the general literature in the field.

Probably the simplest introduction to the main features of the Labour Party history is Henry Pelling's *A Short History of the Labour Party*. This should be supplemented with R. T. McKenzie's now classic account of the organization of and distribution of power within the Party in his book, *British Political Parties*. S. H. Beer's book *Modern British Politics* is an indispensable work which complements some general themes raised by McKenzie but also deals in an extremely stimulating way with a number of aspects of Party policy and ideology.

In education, S. J. Curtis's *Education in Britain since 1900* would serve as a comprehensive, if somewhat dry, introduction to the history of educational administration in Britain in this period. Three books from educational sociologists provide the most interesting analysis of educational issues. The reader *Education, Economy and Society* by Halsey, Floud and Anderson is another classic in its field which deals with some of the most important general themes of the role of the education system in contemporary society. *Parity and Prestige in English Secondary Education* by Olive Banks is a fascinating sociological

SUGGESTIONS FOR FURTHER READING

account of some of the main issues in the development of the English Secondary system. William Taylor in *The Secondary Modern School* deals more specifically with some post-1944 issues and in particular contains a valuable examination of the debate about the 'depressed element' in English education. Although it is now dated, P. E. Vernon's *Selection in Secondary Education* is still a good introduction to the problems of selection in education. And finally, Robin Pedley in *The Comprehensive School* provides probably the best general account of the aims, organization and practice of comprehensive education.

Bibliography

A. OFFICIAL REPORTS AND PAPERS (in chronological order)

The 1918 Education Act.

The Departmental Committee Report on Scholarships and Free Places, Cmd. 968, London: HMSO, 1921.

Report of the Committee on National Expenditure (Geddes Report), Cmnd. 1581, HMSO, 1922.

Report of the Consultative Committee on the Education of the Adolescent (Hadow Report), HMSO, 1926.

Report of the Committee on Private Schools and Other Schools not in Receipt of Grants from Public Funds, HMSO, 1932.

The 1936 Education Act.

Report of the Consultative Committee on Secondary Education (Spens Report), HMSO, 1938.

Report of the Committee on the Public Schools and the General Education System (Fleming Report), HMSO, 1942.

Report of the Committee of the Secondary School Examinations Council (Norwood Report), HMSO, 1943.

White Paper: *Educational Reconstruction*, Cmnd. 6458, HMSO, 1943.

The 1944 Education Act.

Secondary Education: Report of the Advisory Council on Education in Scotland, Cmnd. 7005, HMSO, 1947.

BIBLIOGRAPHY

Early Leaving: A Report of the Central Advisory Council for Education (England) (Gurney-Dixon Report), HMSO, 1954.

15 to 18: A Report of the Central Advisory Council for Education (England) (Crowther Report), HMSO, 1959.

Half Our Future: A Report of the Central Advisory Council for Education (England) (Newsom Report), HMSO, 1963.

Report of the Committee on Higher Education (Robbins Report), HMSO, 1963.

Hansard, 1918-65.

Board of Education:
  Annual Reports, 1918-44.
  Administrative Circulars, 1918-44.

Ministry of Education:
  Annual Reports, 1945-65.
  Administrative Circulars, 1945-65.
  The Nation's Schools, Pamphlet No. 1, HMSO, 1945.
  The New Secondary Education, Pamphlet No. 9, HMSO, 1947.

B. LABOUR PARTY MATERIAL

Minutes and Memoranda of the Advisory Committee on Education, 1918-44.

Local Government Memoranda.

Labour Annual Conference Reports, 1906-65.

Pamphlets on Education (in chronological order):
  Labour and the New Social Order, 1918.
  Unemployment, 1921.
  Boys and Girls, 1924.
  The Broad High Road in Education, 1924.
    Labour's Great Record, 1924.
  The New Spirit in Education, 1924.
  Education of Children over 11, 1925.

Full Speed Ahead—The Labour Government's Education Policy, 1930.
Two Years' Progress, 1931.
Labour and Education, 1934.
The Children's Charter, 1937.
Socialism and Peace, 1938.
Labour's Home Policy, 1945.
Advance in Education, 1947.
Labour Party Speaker's Handbook, 1948-9.
Labour Believes in Britain, 1949.
Labour and the New Society, 1950.
A Policy for Secondary Education, 1951.
The Welfare State, 1952.
Challenge to Britain, 1953.
Speaker's Notes on Labour's Education Policy for England and Wales, 1953.
Tory Record on Education, Housing and Wealth, 1955.
Towards Equality, 1956.
Learning to Live, 1958.
Labour's Education Policy, 1959.
Signposts for the Sixties, 1961.

C. NEWSPAPERS AND JOURNALS CONSULTED

The Times.
(Manchester) Guardian.
Times Educational Supplement.
The Schoolmaster.
Education.
Journal of Education.
New Statesman.
Tribune.
Socialist Commentary.
Labour Party Press Cutting Service, Transport House.

D. UNPUBLISHED THESES

THOMAS, G. M., 'The Development of the Idea of Multilateral Schools in England', 1950. MA Thesis, University of London.

SCHOFIELD, JACK, 'Education and the Labour Movement, 1900-1930', 1960. MEd Thesis, University of Manchester.

E. BOOKS AND ARTICLES ON SOCIALISM AND EDUCATION

ABRAMS, M., ROSE, R., and HINDEN, R. (1960), *Must Labour Lose?*, London: Penguin.

ATTLEE, C. (1937), *The Labour Party in Perspective*, London: Gollancz.

ARMFELT, R. (1955), *The Structure of English Education*, London: Cohen & West.

BANKS, O. (1955), *Parity and Prestige in English Secondary Education*, London: Routledge & Kegan Paul.

BARNARD, H. C. (1952), *A Short History of English Education, 1760-1944*, London: University of London Press.

BEER, MAX (1919), *A History of British Socialism*, Vol. 1, London: Bell.

BEER, S. H. (1965), *Modern British Politics*, London: Faber & Faber.

BRAND, C. F. (1965), *The British Labour Party*, London: Oxford University Press.

BUTLER, R. A. (1952), 'Education: the View of a Conservative', *Yearbook of Education*, London: University of London, Institute of Education.

CLARKE, F. (1943), *Education and Social Change*, London: The Sheldon Press.

COLE, M. (1954), *What is a Comprehensive School?*, London: London Labour Party.

COLE, G. D. H. (1948), *A History of the Labour Party from 1914*, Routledge & Kegan Paul.

BIBLIOGRAPHY

— (1952), 'Education and Politics', *Yearbook of Education*, University of London, Institute of Education.
— (1952), *Essays on Social Theory*, London: Macmillan.
— (1935), *The Simple Case for Socialism*, Gollancz.
COLLIER, K. G. (1958), *The Social Purposes of Education*, Routledge & Kegan Paul.
CONANT, J. B. (1953), *Education and Liberty*, New York: Harvard University Press.
— (1948), *Education in a Divided World*, Oxford University Press.
CRICK, B. (1960), 'Socialist Literature in the 50s', *Political Quarterly*.
CROSLAND, C. A. R. (1962), *The Conservative Enemy*, London: Cape.
— (1956), *The Future of Socialism*, Cape.
CROSSMAN, R. H. (ed.) (1952), *New Fabian Essays*, London: Turnstile Press.
— (1965), *Planning for Freedom*, London: Hamish Hamilton.
CURTIS, S. J. (1952), *Education in Britain since 1900*, London: A. Dokers.
DENT, H. C. (1946), *A New Order in English Education*, University of London Press.
— (1954), GROWTH IN ENGLISH EDUCATION, *1946-52*, Routledge & Kegan Paul.
— (1949), *Secondary Education for All*, Routledge & Kegan Paul.
DOBINSON, C. H. (ed.) (1951), *Education in a Changing World*, Oxford University Press.
DURBIN, EVAN (1940), *The Politics of Democratic Socialism*, Routledge & Kegan Paul.
ELVIN, H. L. (1965), *Education and Contemporary Society*, London: C. A. Watts.
English New Educational Fellowship, (1950), *The Comprehensive School*, London.

BIBLIOGRAPHY

FLOUD, J. (1957), *Social Class and Educational Opportunity*, London: Heinemann.

GLASIER, J. B. (1921), *The Meaning of Socialism*, London: J.L.P. Publishing Dept.

GRAVES, J. (1943), *Policy and Progress in Secondary Education, 1902-1942*, London: Nelson.

GRAY and MOSHINSKY (1938), 'Ability and Opportunity in English Education', in HOGBEN, L., *Political Arithmetic*, London: Allen & Unwin.

HALSEY, A. H. (1961), *Ability and Educational Opportunity*, London: OECD.

— et al. (1961), *Education, Economy and Society*, New York: Free Press of Glencoe.

— and GARDNER, L. (March 1953), 'Selection for Secondary Education and Achievement in Four Grammar Schools', *British Journal of Sociology*.

HEARNSHAW, F. J. C. (1928), *Survey of Socialism*, Macmillan.

HOLMES, B. (1956), 'The Reform of English Education—The 1944 Education Act', *Yearbook of Education*, University of London, Institute of Education.

HORRABIN, J. F. and HORRABIN, W. (1924), *Working Class Education*, Labour Publishing Co.

HUSEN, T. and HENRYSSON, S. (eds.) (1958), *Differentiation and Guidance in the Comprehensive School*, London: Almquist & Wiksell.

JAMES, ERIC (1951), *Education and Leadership*, London: Harrap.

JAY, DOUGLAS (1902), *Socialism in the New Society*, London: Longmans.

JENKINS, ROY (1959), *The Labour Case*, Penguin.

JUDGES, A. V. (1965), *Looking Forward in Education*, London: Faber & Faber.

— 'The Educational Influence of the Webbs', *British Journal of Sociology*, Vol. X, p. 33.

— (1953-4), 'Tradition and the Comprehensive School', *British Journal of Educational Studies*, Vol. II, i.

KANDEL, I. (1931), *History of Secondary Education*, Harrap.

— (1933), *Studies in Comparative Education*, Harrap.

LEESE, J. (1950), *Personalities and Power in English Education*, London: Arnold.

LEYBOURNE, G., and WHITE, K. (1940), *Education and the Birth Rate*, Cape.

LINDSAY, K. (1926), *Social Progress and Educational Waste*, Routledge & Kegan Paul.

LOWNDES, G. A. N. (1937), *The Silent Social Revolution*, Oxford University Press.

MACDONALD, J. R. (1905), *Socialism and Society*, I.L.P. Publishing Dept.

MACK, E. C. (1941), *Public Schools and Public Opinion*, London: Methuen.

MCKENZIE, R. T. (1955), *British Political Parties*, Heinemann.

MANNHEIM, K., and STEWART, W. A. C. (1962), *An Introduction to the Sociology of Education*, Routledge & Kegan Paul.

MAYS, J. B. (1962), *Education and the Urban Child*, Liverpool: Liverpool University Press.

MILIBAND, R. (1956), *Parliamentary Socialism*, Allen & Unwin.

MILLER, T. W. G. (1961), *Values in the Comprehensive School*, Birmingham: University of Birmingham Institute of Education.

MUSGRAVE, P. W. (1965), *The Sociology of Education*, Methuen.

NATIONAL ASSOCIATION OF LABOUR TEACHERS (1947), *The Comprehensive School*, London.

NATIONAL UNION OF TEACHERS (1958), *Inside the Comprehensive School*, London.

OTTOWAY, A. K. C. (1955), *Education and Society*, Routledge & Kegan Paul.

PEDLEY, R. (1956), *Comprehensive Education*, Gollancz.
— 1963), *The Comprehensive School*, Penguin.
PELLING, H. (1961), *A Short History of the Labour Party*, Macmillan.
— (1961), *The Origins of the Labour Party, 1880-1900*, Macmillan.
PETERSON, A. D. C. (1957), *Educating Our Rulers*, London: Duckworth.
PRING, BERYL (1937), *Education: Capitalist and Socialist*, Methuen.
SHANKS, M. (1960), 'Labour Philosophy and the Current Position', *Political Quarterly*.
SIMON, BRIAN (1965), *Education and the Labour Movement, 1870-1920*, London: Lawrence & Wishart.
— (1953), *Intelligence Testing and the Comprehensive School*, London: Lawrence & Wishart.
— (1954), *The Common Secondary School*, London: Lawrence & Wishart.
— (ed.) (1957), *New Trends in English Education*, London: MacGibbon & Kee.
SMITH, H. P. (1956), *Labour and Learning*, Oxford: Blackwell.
STEVENS, FRANCES (1960), *The Living Tradition*, London: Hutchinson.
TAWNEY, R. H. (1924), *Education: the Socialist Policy*, I.L.P. Publishing Dept.
— (1931), *Equality*, Allen & Unwin.
— (1922), *Secondary Education for All*, Allen & Unwin.
— (1964), *The Radical Tradition*, Allen & Unwin.
TAYLOR, A. J. P. (1965), *English History, 1914-1945*, Oxford University Press.
TAYLOR, WILLIAM (1963), *The Secondary Modern School*, London: Faber & Faber.
TRACEY, H. (1925), *The Book of the Labour Party*, London: Caxton Publishing Co.

BIBLIOGRAPHY

TRUBRIDGE, R. W. (1947), *The Multilateral School*, private publication.

ULAM, A. (1950), *The Philosophical Foundations of English Socialism*, Harvard University Press.

VAIZEY, J. (1966), *Education for Tomorrow*, Penguin.

— (1958), *The Costs of Education*, Allen & Unwin.

VERNON, P. E. (1942), *Selection in Secondary Education*, University of London Press.

WILKINSON, R. (1964), *The Prefects*, Oxford University Press.

WILLEY, F. T. (1964), *Education Today and Tomorrow*, London: Michael Joseph.

WILSON, H. (1964), *The New Britain*, Penguin.

— (1964), *The Relevance of British Socialism*, London: Weidenfeld & Nicolson.

WILSON, J. (1962), *Public Schools and Private Practice*, Allen & Unwin.

YOUNG, MICHAEL (1958), *The Rise of the Meritocracy*, London: Thames & Hudson.